Judah,

—

Back Upright

Skull & Bones, Knights Templar, Freemasons

&

The Bible

Sacred Scroll of Seven Seals Series: Book II
[This series can be read in any order.]

Truth Flasher Books

Copyright © 2018 All rights reserved.

This book or any portion thereof may not be reproduced or used in any manner whatsoever without the express written permission.

Printed in the United States of America
First Printing, 2018
ISBN: 9781976940163
Crown King, Arizona
You may correspond with the Author of this work at the following url (below):

JudahVisionMail@Gmail.com

Table of Contents I

Title Page

Copyright Page

Table of Contents

Introduction

Warning

1—The Michelangelo Code

2—Nimrod

3—Babel

4—The Lost Knowledge of Good and Evil

5—Satanism

6—'Highest Satanic Holiday'

7—Ancient Mystery Religion

8—Father of Nations

9—God vs 'The Gods'

10—Killing Kids

11—Sacrifice

12—Tower to 'the gods'

13—Twelve Tribes

14—Pillars of Cloud and Fire

15—First King of Judah

16—Temple of Doom

17—Jerusalem

Table of Contents II

18—Solomon

19—The System of the Beast

20—Daniel's Empirical Prophecy

21—I Head of Gold—Babylon

22—II Medo-Persia—the Writing on the Wall

23—III - IV—Greece / Rome

24—Dead Sea Scrolls

25—Daniel and the Ishtar Gate

26—King of Kings

27—Where 'Iron' Meets 'Clay'

28—Constantine

29—Human Sacrifice

30—Legs of Iron

31—Verginia, USA

32—Revolution 9:11

33—Predictive Programming

34—Revelation 2:7

35—Counterfeit New Jerusalem

36—The Threshing Floor

37—Amazing Grace

38—Jedidiah Knights

Poem—Chopped Sticks

Introduction

We tune in to the evening news and listen as our 'evolved' American government names great aircraft after satanic figures such as the Biblical 'Nimrod.' We name **gigantic** bombs after wicked tribes of **'giants'** : 'MOAB'—**M**other **O**f **A**ll **B**ombs—*the largest non-nuclear bomb ever built.* We even name our invented enemies after ancient devils such as 'Isis,' and 'Geronimo,' and we name missions for villains like 'Neptune.' We then use these implements of destruction to spill the same blood in the same war zones as these same bloodlines have been doing *since Biblical times!* I could go on-and-on, and, yet, very few of us even recognize these acts as evil.

But with an armchair understanding of the Holy Chronicles you too will realize that our 'leaders' take a lot more stock in this Book than anyone had ever realized; they know the slight nuances of the Holy Text like they do their own children but look at you straight-faced and deem it all a 'lie.' Or, worse yet, they impersonate Christians and shout falsehoods from our idle pulpits to rob the tender of the 'meek.'

While most books on the philosophy of *Good* and *Evil* dismantle only a couple of verses from individual Biblical events and their relevance reduced to semantical meaning, my role has become that of threading these accounts together chronologically; I will demonstrate to you in everyday speak that every single empire from the dawn of man was predicted in this Holy Book; whether you believe in it now, *or not*. A high-speed overview of the order and significance of the events, themselves, rather than the former will demonstrate a continuous theme which flows through the Bible and right into your living room in the form of today's news headlines. *That is*, if you know what to look for.

This 'high-speed overview of the entire Bible' brings into focus a single Bible 'Story.' The amazing account begins with Adam and Eve and continues today in the midst of a tribulation which, due to the level of deceit, *no one even sees*. The following text will track a savage bloodline of vikings, who sieged Britain in the *Norman Invasion,* back to the Knights Templar, to the vile Hebrew Kings of Judah. Believe it or not, we will begin with Prince William and track his bloodline all the way back through Solomon and David, deep into the dark voids of human history. We will even identify their precious 'Holy' Grail which was hidden in plain sight within the text of the King James Bible.

'God's Word' was written thousands of years ago by ancient 'whistleblowers' who brilliantly encrypted the revelation of a 'ruthless conspiracy,' in the words of *JFK who no one even heard*. This timeworn collusion has crossed the thresholds of time, space, culture, language, trade, religion, and great bodies of water. Whether you're an atheist, a satanist, a new-ager, Muslim, Hindu, Buddhist, Christian, *or just confused*, you will walk away from the next 4-or-so hours having *100%* picked a side; and you will be *quite* firm in your beliefs, *no matter which path you've chosen.*

Prepare to crawl out of the dark cave of deceit and into the world of the 'Upright.' For today I will shake the very foundations of your entire belief system.

Once again,

'Enjoy the warm Sunshine!'

Judah!

Warning:

I've entrusted you with the following text with great trembling as I am quite aware of the curses which The Bible places on molesters of God's Word. Let it be known that the many parallels between the scriptures and the news events herein *could* merely reflect clandestine groups using Biblical events and symbolism with which to try and *force* the fulfillment of the Prophecies in this incredible Book.

But, as you will now witness for yourself, this has been a common occurrence throughout history and many of these prophecies fit the grooves of time with great accuracy! I stand in awe of The Bible's great ability to predict every major event in the history of mankind.

It is important that you study The Bible with your own discernment in decision of your beliefs. The only scriptures which I wish to demonstrate their meaning definitively are John 3:16 and the *Ten Commandments* which *must* be followed to prevent the dreadful things documented in this work from occurring in our own society; *though I am afraid it might already be too late*. Other than that, please approach the powerful ideas which you are about to receive with the same caution with which they were written.

Enjoy!

1. The Michelangelo Code

Many consider the Sistine Chapel on which Michelangelo toiled for four years in the early 16th century to be a 'bridge' between the Roman Catholic Church and the Jewish faith. According to a book titled, *The Sistine Secrets: Unlocking the Codes in Michelangelo's Defiant Masterpiece*—written by Rabbi Benjamin Blech and Roy Doliner—the poses of the subjects in Michelangelo's paintings represent Hebrew letters. For example: The two claim that the figures of *David* and the giant *Goliath* form the shape of the letter gimel, which symbolizes g'vurah, or strength; as you can imagine, there is much controversy surrounding these hidden 'clues.'

But one clue for which no such argument can be made is hidden in Michelangelo's depiction of the *Cumaean Sibyl* : In this work, Michelangelo added the infamous '**sixth knuckle**' to the muscular lady-**giant's** left fist. The verse below will explain the meaning of this beast of burden's muscular man-arms, large stature, and extra digits. It is not important that you memorize the information below, just enjoy reading about the giants in our ancient past and absorb the bold-lettered information which outlines the fact that Michelangelo's 'Sibyl' *was* a giantess with **six fingers and six toes**. II Samuel 21 :

King James Version (KJV)

19 And there was again a battle in Gob with the Philistines, where Elhanan the son of Jaareoregim, a Bethlehemite, slew the brother of **Goliath the Gittite, the staff of whose spear was like a weaver's beam**.

20 And there was yet a battle in Gath, where was a man of great stature, **that had on every hand six fingers, and on every foot six toes, four and twenty in number; and he also was born to the giant**.

21 And when he defied Israel, Jonathan the son of Shimeah the brother of David slew him.

22 These four were born to the giant in Gath, and fell by the hand of David, and by the hand of his servants.

As you can see, the 'giants' described in the scripture above share this genetic trait, of having six fingers, with Michelangelo's Sibyl.

If you google image the words, 'six fingers,' you will see that *polydactylism*—also known as *Polydactyly* or *Hyperdactyly*—is, interestingly, a congenital physical anomaly in humans; it is *not* considered a 'defect.' This genetic 'anomaly' is surfacing more-and-more among humans. As a matter of fact, if you google image, 'family of 14 who were all born with six fingers and six toes,' you will see for yourself that these Nephilim (giant) traits are returning to the gene-scape of the human race, and that, save for the extra fingers, most of these hands look as normal as yours and mine. This is not to say that these people are 'bad' any more than Shaq is bad simply for being a 'giant,' even if he *is* a braggadocious freemason;

these are merely genetic carryovers from the past which are clearly explained by The Bible.

The first half of the title of Michelangelo's sixth-knuckle-painting of this 'Sibyl'—**Cumaean**—shouts that she *is* in fact a 'giantess'....In countless ancient accounts, these Sibyls were said to be a tribe of women warriors who were genetic leftovers from a tribe of ancient giants. According to first century historian, *Diodorus Siculus, Library of History* 4. 21. 5 :

> "Herakles then moved on from the Tiber [River of Rome], and as he passed down the coast of what now bears the name of Italia (Italy) he came to the **Kumaion (Cumaean) Plain.**' Here, the myths relate, 'there were men of outstanding strength, * **the fame of whom had gone abroad for *lawlessness* and they were called *Gigantes*'** [these 'Gigantes' are giants]."

That the Greek account above mentions that these Cumaean 'giants' were * '**famous**,' corresponds with the Biblical record below which also clearly explains the earliest *appearance* of these 'giants'—Genesis 6:4:

> King James Version (KJV)
> **4** There were giants in the earth in those days; and also after that, when the sons of God came in unto the daughters of men, and they bear children to them, the same became mighty men which were of old, * **men of renown**.

We've since named multiple professional sports teams in honor of these ancient 'Gigantes' ; for example: the New York 'Giants.' *Yale University,* the sinister home of *The Order of Skull and Bones*, *created* American football as we know it, *which explains a lot.* (There will be much more on *The Order of Skull and Bones* later; this idea will come into better focus for us then.) Curiously, *California,* even has a baseball team named for the *parents* of these 'giants' : the Anaheim Angels. Haven't you ever wondered why that is? Remarkably, these 'Giants' too have become quite world 'renown' for their large stature, just as those mentioned in the Biblical account above. California has even named their greatest city after these angelic beings: *Los Angeles*, 'the City of Angels.'

If you think that all of this 'giant' talk is crazy, *you'd be wrong....* '*Giant,*' may not mean what you think: The Bible recorded that Goliath was only 6' 9," and the Hebrews were generally short. This means that *Shaquille O'neal* is 4 inches taller than was Goliath; it also remains that *Yao Ming* would tower a full nine inches above the Biblical 'giant.' (Many translations of The Bible have edited Goliath's height to make it seem that he was taller than he really was in order to discount the fact that the Nephilim genes are again manifesting today; we all may have these genes encoded in our DNA.)

The two evil-looking 'angels' who appear to be making the infamous 'rude gesture' behind the back of the giantess, *Sibyl*—in Michelangelo's famous painting—are telling now that we know that the 'giants' were mutations of the combined genes of humans and fallen angels, or, *demons*. Shone in this light it appears that these two 'fallen angels' are literally throwing 'the bird' at the human race's grimy fate of living with giants, after, *Lucifer—the leader of the fallen angels—*infamously tempted Eve which *caused* the woeful downfall of man.

That Michelangelo names the 'giantess' in his painting 'Sibyl' demonstrates the fact that Michelangelo understood his human-angel-hybrid to hold special occult powers, since a *Sibyl* is a *prophetess*; these tribes of giants practiced the dark arts and were idolaters, murderers, and soothsayers; and they received their prophetic information from the dark side. Curiously, the base word for *Vatican, itself, means 'fortune tellers'*; which to me *could* imply that the vulgarities and 'secret clues' in these works were simply commissioned accouterments to the images. After all, historically, anyone who defied the pope in any way was in danger of losing their head, and the gesture being made by one of the angels, behind the back of the Sibyl, was equivalent to flashing one's middle finger in anger today.

Michelangelo's contemporary, artist, *Vasari*, who had done some fresco painting himself, marveled at the way Michelangelo had held-up physically through the long ordeal, when Vasari stated the following in his book, *Life of Michelangelo* :

> 'He executed the frescoes in great discomfort, having to work with his face looking upwards, which impaired his sight so-badly that he could not read or look at drawings save with his head turned backwards; and this lasted for several months afterwards. I can talk from personal experience about this, since when I painted five rooms in the great apartments of Duke Cosimo's palace, if I had not made a

chair where I could rest my head and relax from time to time, I would never have finished; and, even so, this work so ruined my sight and injured my head that I still feel the effects, and I am astonished that Michelangelo bore all that discomfort so well.'

The countless 'clues' and 'rude gestures' in Michelangelo's Vatican works appear to be quite a deal more than a simple nose-thumbing at the pope, who, supposedly, had ordered the painter to complete this grueling work '*against* Michelangelo's wishes' ; either way, when it was all said and done, his work amounted to around 14,000 square feet of brilliance.

This all sound nuts, I know, but if you have ever heard of the band 'Incubus' and googled the meaning of this creepy word, you will realize that people still believe to be honoring this age old practice of 'mating' with 'demons.' Below is the Google definition of the word, 'incubus' :

in·cu·bus ˈiNGkyəbəs / noun

A male demon believed to have sexual intercourse with sleeping women.

The painting of the *Cumaean Sibyl,* 'lady-giant,' on the ceiling of the Sistine Chapel is but one of countless examples of clues hidden in Michelangelo's reluctant Vatican works, *which should no longer be ignored*. It is a shame that endless volumes on this topic are filled with meaningless words of fiction since there are so many wonderfully obvious clues hiding in plain site, in architecture, artwork, print, and song. This paper will be written based on veritas alone so, we will leave well-structured theory to agents of confusion—*the Dan Browns of the world*—and you and I will move on in truth which, as *you* will soon see, is *far* more compelling.

In this work, we will explore the following burning question: Are the 'giants' *already* 'back?' Every culture cited legends of winged beings, ancient giants, *and* an epic flood; perhaps the 'giants' for which the world was destroyed by the Great Flood have *returned*. Moving forward in the text, we will see what this means for the human race.

Angels

Along with documenting the existence of giants in our past, The Bible—as well as architecture and folklore found around the world—suggests that these Nephilim genes could *also* manifest as 'bird-like' features in the human gene pool (a trait of their fallen-angel-parents) as in the case of Nebuchadnezzar (who we will study in great detail later). In this Biblical account, Nebuchadnezzar—famous king of ancient Babylon—himself began growing these bird-like 'feathers' and 'claws.'

Images and stories depicting these anomalous creatures—today referred to as, 'avian humanoids,' or simply as, 'bird men'—are found on ancient stone reliefs and tablets allover the world. The many and vast archaeological sites of ancient Babylon are littered with stone depictions of beings with angel-like wings whom they referred to as the *Anunnaki*, which literally translates to : 'those who from heaven to earth came.' The Anunnaki were referred to as, 'the gods' ; *Babylon means, 'Gate of god.'*

Roman Emperors were said to be *demigods*—half man half 'god' (fallen angel)—just as were the giants described in Genesis. The Pharaohs did the same. In fact, beginning with King Nimrod of the Tower of Babel account—also said to be a 'giant'—the Babylonian kings, the Hindus, the Chinese, the Japanese—I could go on-and-on from nearly every patch of land—even from the ancient Norse vikings to the present day 'Rocket Man' of North Korea, all thought they were descendants of 'the gods' (the *fallen angels)*.

When Charlie Sheen famously snapped, *he* proclaimed himself to be an 'Adonis'—or, '*god.'* According to popular belief, Adonis was the son of Theias, king of Syria, and Myrrha (also known as Smyrna) who was a 'god' or, a 'fallen angel.' Below is a crazy shortlist of Charlie-Sheen-claims during *his* moment of 'greatness' :

1. 'I got tiger blood, man. My brain…fires in a way that is—I don't know—maybe **not from this particular terrestrial realm.**'
2. 'I'm tired of pretending like I'm not special. I'm tired of pretending like I'm not bitchin', a total freakin' rockstar **from Mars.**'
3. 'I'm sorry, man, but **I've got magic**. I've got poetry in my fingertips. Most of the time—and this includes naps—**I'm an F-18, bro. And I will destroy you in the air**. I will deploy my ordinance to the ground.'

Note: Charlie's father, *Martin Sheen*, was the star of the 1979 cult classic **Apocalypse** *Now;* the soundtrack for this film includes a Classical number by *Wagner. His work,* sometimes called, *Flight of the Valkyries*—the official title being, *'Ride'* of the Valkyries—

was played in the scene in which an Air Cavalry regiment played the song from helicopter-mounted loudspeakers as a form of psychological warfare, and to excite American Troops during an assault on a North Vietnamese-controlled village. This scene is ironic since the **'Valkyries' were originally fallen angelic beings who obeyed the commands of** *Odin*, **the Norse name for** *King Nimrod*. The imagery for this scene uncannily corresponds with Sheen's aforementioned quote 3.

This one is partly for comic relief; but another part of me wonders if, perhaps, there are 'legends' which have been passed down through *Sheen's* famous bloodline. And the amazing list of stars and powerful Hollywood figures who were reaching out to Charlie, at his moment of instability, could substantiate such a situation where Sheen began to risk the reputations of an entire counterculture of people who pass-on these same beliefs in modern times; *so*, was Charlie simply 'the one who got away?'

Below is a list of groups found allover the world who incorporated these angel-like bird 'gods' into their legends; you don't need to memorize the information, I am only demonstrating a theme which appears to be far more than coincidence :

- Tangata manu of Easter Island, often depicted as a Frigate bird/Human hybrid **Valkyries, possibly connected with Freyja of Norse mythology**
- Angels, in all Abrahamic religions; these are the benevolent Angelic beings mentioned in The Bible

- Anunnaki winged gods Anzu/Zu, Siris, and Lammasu/Shedu from Babylonian mythology; these are the 'fallen angels' detailed in The Bible in which the Anunnaki were the enemies of angel and man alike, whose offspring produced 'giants'; *libraries* of records—*the thousands of stone tablets found in Babylonian excavations*—verify these accounts from the 'dark side' of Scripture
- Alkonost, Gamayun, and Sirin from Russian mythology
- Ekek in Philippine mythology is depicted as a humanoid with bird wings and a beak
- Faravahar of Zoroastrianism
- Garuda, eagle-man mount of Vishnu in Hindu mythology, was pluralized into a class of bird-like beings in Buddhist mythology
- The gods Horus and Thoth from Ancient Egyptian mythology were often depicted as humans with the heads of a falcon and an ibis, respectively
- Huitzilopochtli, the 'left-handed hummingbird'—god of the Aztec City of Tenochtitlan
- The Kinnara and Kinnari in South-east Asia, who are half-human, half-bird
- Karura in Japanese folklore
- Lei Gong, a Chinese thunder god, is often depicted as a Garuda-like bird man
- The second people of the world in Southern Sierra Miwok mythology, as reported by Barrett
- Hermes, and his counterpart Mercury in Greek and Roman mythology are usually depicted with sandals and a helm with wings on it, and sometimes also with bird-like wings
- Icarus legend from Greek mythology

- Wayland the Smith legend from Germanic mythology
- Nike, Boreas, Eros and the Gorgon sisters from Greek mythology are all depicted with birdlike wings; also the Sirens and Harpies were often represented as half-human half-bird
- Many of the Native American 'Indians' of North America have legends of bird-man-hybrids; countless tribes adhere feathers to costumes and perform magic dances which have the potential to 'bring rain' among other fulfilled desires, which are granted by their 'feathered gods'
- This one is interesting: the 'Feathered Serpent' is a supernatural deity; the Feathered Serpent is worshipped in much of the Mesoamerican religions; it was called Quetzalcoatl among the Aztecs, Kukulkan among the Yucatec Maya, and Q'uq'umatz and Tohil among the K'iche' Maya; this one is mind-boggling since satan originally appeared in the Garden of Eden as a 'serpent,' combining the image of satan with that of the bird men of the Anunnaki of Ancient Babylon

These amazing tribes of stone-**mason**-giants who worshipped bird-men seem to have been allover the world; they all just had a slight twist on the same ancient Canaanite rituals: *building pyramids, worshipping—and themselves becoming—the 'sun gods,' and killing their own kids.* From cannibals deep inside the jungles of New Guinea to the Egyptian Pharaohs to the Roman Emperors to virgin-tossing islanders who sacrificed people in volcanoes, they all worshiped from these 'pyramids'—aka *towers* or other 'high places' as The Bible calls them—where they *'spoke'* to 'the gods.' It all began with King Nimrod, *inventor* of the pyramid and the first evil king and so called 'god' of the entire world.

The Bible threatens a timeworn scam; *it reveals an ancient secret* for which the veils are about to drop. No matter what you believe now, prepare to discover for yourself why the dust on your Bible—the bestselling book of all time, holding the answer to every mystery in the multiverse—is so thick.

2. Nimrod

Noah's Ark

Before the flood, the men of the earth had adopted such evil in *their* society that God finally became fed-up with their hopeless arrogance and wicked ways, to the point that he destroyed the entire world by water— *The Great Flood*. The 'giants' of the earth—the *Nephilim* described in the Bible—along with all 'flesh' not aboard Noah's boat, were drowned.

Because Noah had maintained his righteousness amongst an entire world of the darkest malevolence ever known, God had given Noah a heads-up concerning the destruction of the world by water. Genesis 6 :

> King James Version (KJV)
>
> **5** And God saw that the wickedness of man was great in the earth, and that every imagination of the thoughts of his heart was only evil continually.
> **6** And it repented the Lord that he had made man on the earth, and it grieved him at his heart.
> **7** And the Lord said, I will destroy man whom I have created from the face of the earth; both man, and beast, and the creeping thing, and the fowls of the air; for it repenteth me that I have made them.

8 But Noah found grace in the eyes of the Lord.

So Noah became the laughing stock of his time as his community watched him construct the world's first ocean liner/cargo ship, probably *nowhere near a great body of water.* After '40 days and forty nights' of rain, *Noah*, his family—*Noah's wife, 3 sons and their wives*—and the animals, all aimlessly bobbled in the ocean for around 5 months. Finally the waters receded and Noah released the animals; can you imagine the smell that came out of that thing?

This group of 8, *the only people now left on the planet*, migrated right down the valley from where Noah's great cargo ship was beached at the top of *Mount Ararat* and found themselves in the 'land of Shinar.' *Shinar* was an abundant land since it was conveniently located between two rivers, the *Tigres* and the *Euphrates*. We now know *Shinar* as Ancient Mesopotamia. From Noah's small family, a whole new **civilization** took root. This area is now referred to by academics as the '**Cradle** of **Civilization**,' since they cannot deny that **Shinar *is* the location of man's origin**. *Today it is known as Iraq.*

The new Civilization would come to be known as *Babylon,* and Noah's great-grandson would go on to be *King Nimrod* of this empire—the first *World* Empire. Nimrod as you already know was an 'evil' king—*the worst*. Many believe that the 'man of perdition'—'antichrist'—spoken-of by end times scholars would be a genetic resurrection of Nimrod's actual DNA. This *could* explain the hasty 'archeological digs' for 'mummies' in the area; perhaps the sons of darkness were looking for *'the beast'*—the *'Abaddon'* of Revelation—in order to revive his DNA. The Greek name for 'the beast,' Ἀπολλύων'—Apollyon, or, Apollo—means, *the Destroyer!* Get this, the monster being discussed is described in, *Revelation...wait for it......'9:11!' Soon I will reveal to you that these creeps wouldn't necessarily need to isolate anyone's DNA in order to conjure up evil from the past.*

The earliest story ever recorded in stone by man—*the Epic of **Gilgamesh***—is a tribute to 'Nimrod.' The gist of this mythical version of the flood outlines a 'giant,' standing 18 feet tall, who had 'saved himself from a great flood.' This very first fictional narrative—'story'—would set the framework for Greek Mythology and all of the other half-truth counterfeits of The Bible (the 'false' religions). Many ancient rabbinical accounts of Nimrod also record that Nimrod was a 'giant' ; some scholars even speculate that Nimrod had somehow found a way to resurrect the 'Nephilim' DNA *in his own blood.* He was indeed a large man if you go by the stone inscriptions found allover Babylon. In every image, he is head and shoulders above the surrounding people.

There are literally tons of writings about this ancient giant, 'man of renown.' So there is no 'guessing' about this guy; the information is all there and carefully documented in every culture around the world. This man is still worshipped *everywhere*, even by you, unknowingly, with all of our pagan holidays—they *all* go back to Nimrod—in fact, Christmas is *Nimrod's* birthday, *not 'Christ's.'* And perhaps the materialistic orgy that Christmas has become is exactly why Christ *didn't* make mention of *His* special day.

It is said that Nimrod was a great hunter—in Genesis—and even a hunter of mens' souls, in the Rabbinical writings of the Talmud. Nimrod was the first known inventor of atheism. The Jewish Talmud states that Nimrod had 'beheaded god' in the mountains. After which, he returned from this ominous hunting trip and announced to his people: 'I beheaded God in the mountains but, don't worry. It's okay, everyone…because I'll be your *new* god, now!'

'Darwinism' (survival of the fittest), has accomplished the exact same mission, 'killing God,' but just with a high-tech twist. Now, in the same world where the *laws of thermodynamics, physics*, and the rest of the laws of *science don't allow for anything to be created from 'nothing*,' we all believe that everything, including us, *were*. After he 'killed God,' his people bowed down to Nimrod and this system of mayhem was born.

Nimrod was very prolific with public human sacrifice and the social climate of his times consisted of endless, godless rituals and everyday debauchery, public and otherwise, just as in the days of the flood. The Bible says that Noah's offspring were genetically free from the corrupted seed of the 'Nephilim'—the evil for which the whole world had just been destroyed by water—but it didn't say anything about the purity of the bloodline of Noah's sons' wives. We now know that there *was* evil aboard that boat.

It is important to remember that *Nimrod* was the *first* 'man of perdition' world leader. And regardless of the final mechanism, Nimrod *is* the very prototype for the evil one who will rise up in the end and proclaim himself to be *'God'*—in our own times!

3. Babel

Nimrod could be attributed to the invention of nearly every aspect of our society. But, perhaps Nimrod's most infamous accomplishment was the invention of the *skyscraper*, which in the account is referred to as a 'Tower.' Genesis 11 :

> King James Version (KJV)
>
> **1**1 And the whole earth was of **one language**, and of **one speech**.
>
> **2** And it came to pass, as they journeyed from the east, that they found a plain in the land of Shinar; and they dwelt there.
>
> **3** And they said one to another, Go to, let us make brick, and burn them thoroughly. And they had brick for stone, and slime had they for morter.
>
> **4** And they said, Go to, let us build us a city and a tower, whose top may reach unto heaven; and let us make us a name, lest we be scattered abroad upon the face of the whole earth.
>
> **5** And the Lord came down to see the city and the tower, which the children of men builded.
>
> **6** And the Lord said, Behold, **the people is one**, and **they have all one language**; and this they begin to do: and **now nothing will be restrained from them, which they have imagined to do.**

7 Go to, let us go down, and there confound their language, that they may not understand one another's speech.
8 So the Lord scattered them abroad from thence upon the face of all the earth: and they left off to build the city.

The 'Tower of Babel' has wrongfully been depicted in paintings as a conical structure, with a spiral staircase around its perimeter. Believe it or not, **today's European Union's 'Parliament Building' is designed after Pieter Bruegel the Elder's artful depiction of Babel**, painted in 1563. These tower renditions couldn't be further from the truth. The 'Tower of Babel' was a 'Ziggurat'—what we now refer to as a 'stepped pyramid.' It was not much different, in shape, than the 'Great Pyramids' at Giza. The only real difference is, the pyramid of Babel was a 'stepped pyramid' with a ramped staircase leading to its top, where one would 'speak to the gods.'

The purpose for this 'Tower' fib was intended to distract you from the archeological scent-trail of these 'pyramids' which now litter every corner of earth, in every single society. The truth of the 'pyramids,' if it were spelled-out for you, would lend credence to the Biblical account of Nimrod; *the dots would begin to connect more easily*. This building was an abomination used to worship the evil one and elevate the leader of the society—King Nimrod in this case—to the status of 'the gods.' Today 'pyramids' have evolved into the 'skyscrapers' which we see at the heart of every city.

Many say the Tower served as a metaphor for technology since, technology as well as architecture thrives in this sort of empirical society; slaves produce more than just masonic constructs, it is the combined focused energy of a 'work force' that propels technology, too.

4. The Lost Knowledge of Good and Evil

'*Evil*,' is now the ripe 'fruit' of a wicked seed planted eons ago after dripping from the chins of your earliest ancestors. We *still* pucker from this bitter fruit, hastily plucked from the *'Tree of the Knowledge of Good and Evil' so long ago*—it's the *'Forbidden Fruit,'* which was tasted by man and woman thousands of years ago. Below is this account from the first book of The Bible, Genesis 3 :

> King James Version (KJV)
> **3** Now the serpent was more subtil than any beast of the field which the Lord God had made. And he said unto the woman, Yea, hath God said, Ye shall not eat of every tree of the garden?
> **2** And the woman said unto the serpent, We may eat of the fruit of the trees of the garden:
> **3** But of the fruit of the tree which is in the midst of the garden, God hath said, Ye shall not eat of it, neither shall ye touch it, lest ye die.
> **4** And the serpent said unto the woman, Ye shall not surely die:
> **5 * For God doth know that in the day ye eat thereof, then your eyes shall be opened, and ye shall be as gods, knowing good and evil.**

The bold section * **is the knowledge that we could ourselves be 'the gods' of this world**. Dominion over the animals just wasn't enough for these two. Like King Nimrod who built his tower to 'the heavens,' Adam and Eve must have been the *first* humans who longed to be supreme leaders of *intelligent* creatures: *other men*—their descendants. But the scam would only work if these two geniuses would deny their maker, *causing them to* '*die.*' This is the same exact message Yeshua (Jesus Christ—explained later) spread: No Yeshua…*No* Life! Look at Genesis 3:22 :

> **22** And the Lord **God said, Behold, the man is become as one of us**, to know good and evil: and now, **lest he put forth his hand, and take also of the tree of life**, and eat, **and live for ever**:

It is true. Partaking of the 'knowledge of good and evil' *would* cause 'death' as the serpent had implied, but, *for the chance of being a 'god!'* According to The Bible, man's life spanned nearly a thousand years back then so, I can hear the two, now; here is how I imagine this conversation going: 'A millennium sounds like an *eternity* to me. So, what does it matter if we die and disappear after all that time has passed?' And in my mind, I can even see the pair working out the math on their fingers.

But, in Genesis 6, we see that God had pulled the rug out from under Adam and Eve's unsuspecting relatives, during the 'days' of the 'giants'— right before the flood—when God limits our lifespan to 120 years. Genesis 6 :

3 And the Lord said, My spirit shall not always strive with man, for that he also is flesh: yet **his days shall be an hundred and twenty years**.

This whole becoming 'god' trick probably sounded like a good idea, despite certain death, 'in the beginning' when man lived a thousand years but, the deceit would've been so thick by this time that there was no going back when lifespan was limited to 120 years. 'Pandora's Box' had already been opened. All of the lies and 'mystery religions' would've multiplied incredibly, by this time. Even 'the gods' (emperors, Pharaohs, kings, etc.) wouldn't have been 100% sure of their true origin and history after the tsunamis of lies had already completely covered them. I am sure that, just like our leaders today, they truly thought that they *were* our 'gods.'

The Scriptures below show a parallel between King Nimrod's city-building—*human farming*—and the Adam and Eve account, demonstrating that elevation of one's status to that of 'the gods' *is* the ever-mysterious 'original sin.' Genesis 1 :

> King James Version (KJV)
> **27** So God created man in his own image, in the image of God created he him; male and female created he them.
> **28** And God blessed them, and **God said unto them, Be fruitful, and multiply, and replenish the earth**…

In direct violation to God's orders in bold—'**replenish the earth**'—these two must have stacked their offspring like chord wood so *they* could serve as 'the gods.' We do the same today. Only 3% of the earth's dry land is actually populated; the rest is being 'preserved.' This is an ancient scam with which our 'inheritance' has been stolen; the Paris Climate Agreement is part of the same fascist lie being used to close this sphere of despotism. This ancient scam was designed to inflate property values, create social classism—*hierarchy, the mechanism which allows a single leader to rise up and rule the world*—and control individuals *in every way*.

5. Satanism

According to Anton Szandor Lavey's '*satanic* bible,' we can all be little 'gods' on earth. Here is one of the suggested rituals described in the satanic bible—the 'book of lucifer'—in which you probably, unknowingly, already even partake.

And now, **'satanism' made as easy as 1—2—3**. Below is Lavey's **first 'step' toward worshipping the devil** :

The satanist feels: 'Why not really be honest and if you are going to create a god in your image, why not create that god as yourself.' Every man is a god if he chooses to recognize himself as one. So, the Satanist celebrates his own birthday as the most important holiday of the year. After all, aren't you happier about the fact that you were born than you are about the birth of someone you have never even met? Or for that matter, aside from religious holidays, why pay higher tribute to the birthday of a president or to a date in history than we do to the day we were brought into this greatest of all worlds? **Despite the fact that some of us may not have been wanted, or at least were not particularly planned**, we're glad, even if no one else is, that we're here! **You should give yourself a pat on the back, buy yourself whatever you**

want, treat yourself like the king (or god) that you are, and generally celebrate your birthday with as much pomp and ceremony as possible.

To make someone feel rejected or unwanted and to pander-to and nurture those innate, infantile emotions, in order to make an individual feel wanted and accepted, is brainwashing 101. This new *god starter kit* is preceded by the following claim :

'The highest of all holidays in the Satanic religion is the date of one's own birthday.'

If you still aren't convinced of the existence of this evil system, here is a little tidbit right from the website of the 'church of satan' which should clear things up nicely for you. Below is **Step 2 toward worshipping the devil** :

Satanists are atheists. We see the universe as being indifferent to us, and so all morals and values are subjective human constructions. Our position is to be self-centered, **with ourselves being the most important person (the "God") of our subjective universe**, so **we are sometimes said to worship ourselves**.

This age-old trick is just another mechanism with which to 'kill' God and elevate *yourself* to a godlike status; just as did Nimrod. This recruiting website for the antichrist goes on to verify our suspicions even more clearly when it remarks :

Our current High Priest Gilmore calls this **the step moving from being an atheist to being an "I-Theist."**

And though the 'satanist' claims simply to be 'worshipping self,' the **'stepped'** system described above is clearly a slow brainwashing technique with which to invite 'evil' into your life. Once this step is taken, you have filled your spiritual vessel with 'evil' which can then manifest in many different ways, with little interruption from the user's former set of values. The use of the word 'step,' *above*, is also telling, since the Tower of Babel account too used a tower to *step* their way to heaven—where a 'god' would live—as does the Jacob's ladder account.

Below is a ***continuation* of step 2 toward 'the heavens'—'worshipping the devil.'** :

—**satanic bible Introduction**
"It is not an easy religion to adopt in a society ruled so long by Puritan ethics. There is no false altruism or mandatory love-thy-neighbor concept in this religion. satanism is a blatantly selfish, brutal philosophy. It is based on the belief that human beings are inherently selfish, violent creatures, that **life is a Darwinian struggle for survival of the fittest, that only the strong survive and the earth will be ruled by those who fight to win the ceaseless competition that exists in all jungles—including those of urbanized society.**"
Burton H Wolfe—

The final quote/'step' from the satanic bible, below, will show how this ancient philosophy transitions the human mind from removing god, by yourself *becoming* one of 'the gods,' to chucking your own neighbors into a hot furnace as the 'Nazi' system of antichrist and countless others have done.

Below is **step 3 toward** worshipping the devil—the finality of this high-tech removal of God :

> The person who takes every opportunity to "pick on" others is often mistakenly called "sadistic." In reality, **this person is a misdirected masochist who is working towards his own destruction**. The reason a person viciously strikes out against you is because they are afraid of you or what you represent, or are resentful of your happiness. **They are weak**, insecure, and on extremely shaky ground when you throw your curse, and **they make ideal human sacrifices**.
> **Anton Szandor LaVey—**

Charles Darwin's popular, high-tech version of **this old scam was originally titled**: '*The Origin of Species by Means of Natural Selection*, or the **Preservation of Favoured Races** in the Struggle for Life.' *After* this textual garbage caused the event in Europe known now as the 'holocaust' which resulted in the genocide of millions, the distributors of these lies *rethought* the old title of 'Darwin's' book which was plagiarized to begin with, finally dropping the whole '**Preservation of Favoured Races**' part, in the end.

Isn't it amazing! Here we got a shameless look into the exact antithesis of the Genesis Adam and Eve account, from the other side—the 'Dark Side!' The '***favored races***' part of the title of Darwin's book refers to the descendants of the 'royals' among the Hebrew tribes—*of all colors and nations*—who've ruled the world since Biblical times. Natural selection means that, *you* killed your neighbor or took his belongings simply because he was 'weaker' than you. *Selfishness* perpetuates this scam and the atrocities which you personally commit in the name of greed ultimately keeps your slave masters in power. Everyone, at every level of this system, has *something* to gain—the 'fruit.'

Well, well, well...it appears that **the 'book of lucifer'—satan's most recent *counterfeit* bible—still teaches that you too can be a 'god!'** Although this demonstration of the evil one's own literature illustrates very clearly that you are *not* 'the god' of this sort of society. Just like everything else that comes out of satan's mouth, it is a *lie*, but, we can now be completely sure that this *is* **'the Lost Knowledge of Good and Evil.'**

You may not want to compete in a world where *everyone* is a god, though. Since now the world will simply exist as a huge gladiators arena, where the average individual merely becomes a footstool to the neighbors who are bigger and meaner than you.

You'd better be a real 'tough guy' in the climax of an apocalypse of this proportion. After all, how can the 'satanist' be a good 'magician' capable of tricking his neighbors for personal gain, which *is* the very philosophy of this gross religion, after *everyone* in the society becomes a magician?

Now you must be a *very powerful* 'magician' to compete in this 'dog eat dog world' as 'the satanic bible' puts it. What are the odds of that?

You would probably have the same odds as you do becoming a president or a king now: zero, if you are not in the direct bloodline of *William the Conquerer.* This system only benefits the man on top—'the god.' The god' *at the top of this 'pyramid'* is most likely the leader of 'the fallen angels' : *Lucifer.*

6. 'Highest satanic Holiday'

Before we get started on this section, I would like to disclose that I too celebrated my birthday last year, so I am not judging; I am simply demonstrating the evil origins of this custom as well as the slow social programming of society that can be observed from the history of the birthday celebration.

We have established from the satanic bible itself that one's 'birthday' is the most satanic of holidays. But how when and where did this selfish ritual begin? Unbelievably, history's 'god kings' also began the ritual of worshipping *self* on the day of one's birth—the 'birthday celebration.' Encyclopedia Americana (1991) states :

> 'The ancient world of **Egypt**, **Greece**, **Rome**, and **Persia** celebrated the birthdays of gods, kings, and nobles.'

In another book, *The Lore of Birthdays*, authors *Ralph* and *Adelin Linton* revealed an underlying reason for this, they wrote :

> '**Mesopotamia** and **Egypt**, the **cradles of civilization**, were also the first lands in which men remembered and honoured their birthdays. The keeping of birthday records was important in ancient

times principally because a birth date was essential for the casting of a horoscope.'

'Mesopotamia and Egypt' is academic code for Babylon! 'Babylon' is scarcely used by academics to describe this empire because of its significance to The Bible. Anything which may prove The Bible is discounted. Get excited, though, because ancient Babylon was discovered in recent times and you won't believe how the unfolding events, thereafter, line up with the Words of the Prophets.

Self worship—*Birthdays—began* in Babylon with King Nimrod, the first man to ever rise to the 'god' status of being king of the world; Nimrod was the first king of all mankind! This is the result of this same 'system of antichrist,' or 'satanism.' It is a system where, in its finality, you will be too busy bowing down to the 'image' of whoever is the most heinous member of your society, or *their* pantheon of 'the gods,' to enjoy *your* little 'kingdom' (*your apartment and your dog*, I suppose). *Open* practice of satanism is the final phase—just before human sacrifice—before a society implodes. The *'sodomites'* come just before that.

Here is what the heroic *Phil Robertson*—star of the hit show *Duck Dynasty*—said about this 'system of antichrist,' when being interviewed by Sean Hannity :

> 'No Jesus with Hitler—with the Nazis, *no Jesus*. They wanted to dominate the world and they were famous for murder. The Shintoists came along—no Jesus there, Sean. They were famous for

murder. They wanted to conquer the world. Look at the blood that was spilled with those two. Then comes Communism. No Jesus with them either and they wanted to conquer the world and they slaughtered millions. So you have murder, murder, murder.'

Phil was fired from his show, *Duck Dynasty*, for openly condemning homosexuality in the name of his beliefs. But, due to public outcry, phil was hired back. This, my friend, is a hero, and *that* is a miracle. For in today's social climate, it is far more acceptable to be a satanist or a homosexual than it is to be a Christian.

Looking ahead in the text—in our studies of *Daniel* and other Prophets—we will see this 'system' *at work*. Daniel will offer us a sneak preview of the social climate of the final apocalypse written of in the book of Revelation. It really isn't all that complicated, if you only have the key knowledge which unlocks the powerful book of the future; **or, perhaps it's *our* present**.

7. Ancient Mystery Religion

Would you believe that when your children learn about 'ancient gods' of Greek 'Mythology' they are, literally, learning about ancient satanism?

As part of my spiritual journey, *painfully*—in the name of research and understanding—I read the chronicles from the dark side as well as undergoing my exhaustive examination of The Bible. Insight can sometimes be gained in the strangest of places but I don't suggest reading the satanic bible *to anyone*; it's complete garbage.

And now I will demonstrate that the teachings in your child's classroom are no different from those of Anton Lavey's—founder of the modern-day satanic church :

By threading together the Greek Myths and The Bible, we can make a better assessment of what happened in *our* ancient past. You must bear in mind, though, that, these 'mystery religions' of ancient Rome were really no 'mystery' to the men who wrote the New Testament. These figures would've been indoctrinated with this manure in every aspect of Roman life from entertainment to the daily worship of 'the gods.' Those fortunate enough to have a copy of scriptures and someone who could read them would have had no problems knowing what you and I are just now discovering today. These are the same Greek 'Myths' with which the authors of the second half of The Bible began to piece together this whole apocalyptic puzzle. The voices of the Prophets are screaming at you now from the past! But, unfortunately, these 'screams' will go unheard to those who don't simply open the covers of The Living Word and peep inside.

-Prometheus—a 'Titan,' giant - half 'god' half man—helped to **'shape man out of mud.'** After which, Athena **breathed life into his clay figure**. Below is one of the coolest verses in the entire Bible, which was quite-apparently counterfeited by the Greeks thousands of years after these Bible 'Stories' came into existence. Genesis 2:7 :

> King James Version (KJV)
> 7 And the Lord God **formed man of the dust of the ground**, and **breathed into his nostrils the breath of life**; and man became a living soul.

Prometheus [Nimrod] is who supposedly assigned 'Epimetheus' (Adam of the Bible) **the job of giving the animals their various qualities**, such as swiftness, cunning, strength, fur, and wings. Unfortunately, by the time he got to man, Epimetheus had already doled out all of the 'desired qualities,' so **Prometheus decided to make man stand *upright* as 'the gods'** did, and he then 'gave man fire.'

Aha! Here we are again! The invention of Darwinism, or 'evolution,' and the *caveman* narrative for which the Smithsonian now displays dummies on all-fours with hair glued to them is, really an ancient Roman invention!

It has nothing to do with 'discovery' or any sort of *scientific* method.' And, again...this garbage is more plagiarism of The Bible, the world's undisputed Bestselling book of all time. This is particularly satanic in its very nature since the Biblical account states that man was made in 'God's image' alone; our image has nothing to do with the *animals* as our schools' satanic bibles suggests. This was an intentional slap in the face of YHWH—whose very breath fills your lungs—since Epimetheus had supposedly 'already doled out all of the desired qualities' to the animals. This implies that man was made inferior to even the animals which we know to be a lie.

Look at the corresponding Biblical passage which explains that Adam had *named* all of the animals. Genesis 2 :

> King James Version (KJV)
> 20 And Adam gave names to all cattle, and to the fowl of the air, and to every beast of the field...

A molested version of the *Knowledge of Good and Evil* is also in the satanic Bible handed to little Johnny or Suzy at your local school: Zeus sent Pandora down to earth as a present for the *Adam* of this twisted story: *Epimetheus*. Zeus ordered Epimetheus to marry Pandora, and sent man another little gift along with her: a 'box,' *in later versions* but it was a sealed pottery vase in the first copy of this tale.

Zeus supposedly ordered the pair to never open the box but he also sent the key to Epimetheus. Pandora begged Epimetheus to let her open it, but he wisely declined. One day he took a little nap and she stole the key and opened the box. To her surprise, out flew every woe of mankind which had never even existed to the two: *sicknesses, worries, crimes, hate, envy* and all variety of trouble were released. It was like a swarm of ugliness which filled the earth looking for dark crevices in which to nest. Pandora was extremely remorseful for having opened the terrible box! She tried to capture each malevolent curse but it was far too late; most all of the swarm had already flown away!

In Greek mythology, Prometheus then gave fire to mankind which angered Zeus. 'Zeus' here is satan; and 'Prometheus' *must* be Nimrod. Just as *man* covets God's throne, *satan's* jealousy was the reason he was expelled from heaven in the first place. The Jewish Talmud reveals to us that Nimrod *invented* fire worship! There is also a clear link between Prometheus and *satan* here, since *Lucifer* means *'bringer of light'* in Latin; this is where the torch first began to represent knowledge; *just as in the case of the statue of Liberty*.

So…to punish Prometheus (Nimrod), Zeus (satan) had had 'Prometheus' chained to a rock and every day an eagle flew down to eat his liver. The liver grew back because Prometheus was immortal—and the eagle again returned for the freshly grown liver treat, every day. Below is the Biblical account for this *chained to a rock* symbology in the 'Prometheus' story. I give you…Jude 6 :

King James Version (KJV)

6 And the angels which kept not their first estate, but left their own habitation, he hath reserved in everlasting chains under darkness unto the judgment of the great day.

Prometheus is a *brilliant* analogue for *Nimrod*—and *his* 'system of antichrist'—since the whole 'regenerating liver' theme is a profound metaphor for the rise and fall of evil dictators who pulled the same exact trick in their societies, *throughout history*. It makes one wonder if some sort of system for spiritually resurrecting the demon 'god' of destruction is at play here: An 'antichrist' like Hitler appears, he's eventually overtaken by a *revolution*, and then the evil leader is put to death; only to repeat the whole thing over again. But only, in our case, there will be no coalition of 'allies' to bail *us* out since the entire world will fall 'as one.'

Nearly every Biblical account follows this same theme of oppression by those who ruled the world: They set up this same system of antichrist by *removing* God and proclaiming themselves to be the 'god' of their subjective societies; this includes the account of the Crucifixion, in which, after millennia of pretending to have 'killed God,' they actually achieved their goal of terminating the human flesh of Christ; this was a huge victory for the sons of darkness who, along with the righteous servants of YHWH, had been impatiently waiting on the Messiah's prophetic arrival, for just this purpose (remember, most of the prophetic Scriptures were based on this event).

The Prophets who God chose to warn the societies of their imminent demise passed-on information which was entrusted to them by God. But in most cases these 'warnings' were *not* well-received by neither these oppressors *nor* the people whom the Prophets were attempting to alert. These brave Prophets were persecuted heavily because they threatened the 'god' status of the antichrist du jour. After *you* have the entire snapshot in your view, you too will begin to threaten these magicians.

Below are the 'screams' from *our* particular Prophet, who was called to warn *us* of the *ultimate* antichrist who would return from the distant past— the most horrible antichrist of all time. *'John,' the author of the apocalyptic Book of Revelation,* was imprisoned on the island of Patmos in Greece, for warning his brethren of the exact mess in which we are now shoulders-deep. And since John was now isolated in a cave for his 'rebellion,' he decided he would write those in the future, *us*, instead—*God* had provided the message. John's passage below fits neatly into the grooves of our study, today. Revelation 17 :

> King James Version (KJV)
> 8 **The beast that thou sawest was, and is not**; and **shall ascend out of the bottomless pit**, and go into perdition: and they that dwell on the earth shall wonder, whose names were not written in the book of life from the foundation of the world, when they behold **the beast that was, and is not, and yet** *is*.

8. Father of Nations

Abraham and The Talmud

Just a couple of generations after Noah, the world had again become wicked in their ways. Babylon was in a full satanic uproar but, once again, The Lord found a righteous servant through which to carry-on his perfect plan. *Abraham* was born in the Babylonian City of Ur. King Nimrod and Abraham actually lived in the very same times.

The Babylonian Talmud has King Nimrod and Abraham facing off in an epic battle of *Good* and *Evil*. In this story, Abraham defied Nimrod, the god and leader of all the heathens and idol worshippers of his time, which led to Abraham's being thrown into a fiery furnace typically known for human sacrifice to Moloch. This story is only hinted-to in the *Torah—the Jewish name for the Old Testament*—but has lived-on through the *oral* legacy of the *Talmud*.

The Rabbinical studies of the Jewish, *'Jerusalem Talmud'* were passed on 'orally,' generation-to-generation, finally being documented during 4th century Galilee. Back when people really understood what they said, sacred writings were incredibly dangerous both to its owner and to the rulers of an antichrist society, so ancients really didn't want to be caught in possession of a copy of the Talmud *or* The Torah (The Old Testament). I believe that the early *oral traditions* are the same mechanism which preserved the * **Pentateuch** 'in the beginning.'

> Note: The * **Pentateuch is the first five books of The Bible**: **Genesis, Exodus, Leviticus, Numbers,** and **Deuteronomy**. Nearly every religious person on this planet reads the same creation and human migration account; the 'Story' we are learning now. This means that from 'Creation' to Noah to the Tower of Babel to the Tribes of Israel to the Kings of Judah, they all accept most of the truth that you and I are studying now.

The *'Babylonian Talmud'* was compiled about the year 500. In the Talmud, each 'rabbi' adds their own personal commentary to the Holy Scriptures of *The Torah.* This 'commentary' is held even more sacred than the 'Torah' itself, *which to me doesn't feel right.* It seems that the words of an endless group of all but forgotten 'rabbis,' *playing telephone,* should *not* be held as sacred as *God's* Word.

Abraham
Men have spent endless volumes studying the *promises* and prophecies between the Hebrew people and the 'God of Abraham, Isaac, and Jacob,' so you and I will simply move forward with our study. But just know that, once you grasp an understanding of the account of the subsequent Twelve Tribes of *your* ancestors, you will enjoy reading the many fulfilled prophecies pertaining to the Israelites—*the Twelve Tribes;* there just isn't time to even think about putting it all into perspective for you, now. But the

accuracy with which these things came to pass is no less than mind-numbing.

Below is the Bible passage which outlines God's promise to 'mingle' the then *'Abram's'* seed with the entire world. This is important because today's 'Jewish' teachers have themselves *only* as the 'chosen people' when in fact the promises of the Israelites apply to all of us now, since **the blood of *Abraham* courses through *all* of our veins if you believe *The Bible*, *The Torah*, *or the Quran*; we are *all* Judah**! :

> Genesis 12:1-3King James Version (KJV)
> **12** Now the Lord had said unto Abram, **Get thee out of thy country**, and from thy kindred, and from thy father's house, **unto a land that I will shew thee**:
> **2** And **I will make of thee a great nation, and I will bless thee, and make thy name great**; and thou shalt be a blessing:
> **3** And I will bless them that bless thee, and curse him that curseth thee: and **in thee shall all families of the earth be blessed**.

In verse 12, YHWH says, **Get thee out of thy country,** which shows us that He wanted us out of these evil cities. And the second part in bold tells Abraham that there is a massive amount of new, fertile land on which His people could live but, the system of Nimrod prevented us from taking our place in this 'Promised Land,' and enslaved us instead.

Believe it or not, the Abraham account most-likely even determined the shape of the end of your penis, *if you have one*, and, for some reason,

The Bible still goes ignored....*Whew! Below is a passage where God prescribes circumcision which is still done today. The scriptures foretell that all nations would be mixed with Hebrew blood and that these great warriors would go on to lead these nations as 'Kings.'* Genesis 17 :

King James Version (KJV)

17 And when Abram was ninety years old and nine, the Lord appeared to Abram, and said unto him, I am the Almighty God; walk before me, and be thou perfect.

2 And **I will make my covenant between me and thee, and will multiply thee exceedingly**.

3 And Abram fell on his face: and God talked with him, saying,

4 As for me, behold, my covenant is with thee, and **thou shalt be a father of many nations.**

5 Neither shall thy name any more be called Abram, but **thy name shall be Abraham; for a father of many nations have I made thee.**

6 And **I will make thee exceeding fruitful,** and **I will make nations of thee,** and **kings shall come out of thee.**

7 And I will establish my covenant between me and thee and thy seed after thee in their generations for **an everlasting covenant**, to be a God unto thee, **and to thy seed after thee.**

8 And **I will give unto thee, and to thy seed after thee, the land wherein thou art a stranger**, all the land of Canaan, for an everlasting possession; **and I will be their God.**

9 And God said unto Abraham, **Thou shalt keep my covenant therefore, thou, and thy seed after thee in their generations.**

10 This is my covenant, which ye shall keep, between me and you and thy seed after thee; **Every man child among you shall be circumcised.**
11 And ye shall circumcise the flesh of your foreskin; and it shall be a token of the covenant betwixt me and you.

So, YHWH changed Abram's name to 'Abraham,' meaning 'Father of Many Nations' ; *this prophecy came to pass!* God also mentioned in the above passage that, '**kings shall come out of thee**,' which as you will see, also came to pass! God also changed the name of Abraham's wife from 'Sarai' to 'Sarah': '**Princess**.'

Abram and Sarai were quite old and without children when God made Abram this promise; he was 99 years old and Sarai was barren. So imagine Abram's surprise when YHWH explained the following in Genesis 10— just before the striking of the covenant about which we've already read:

Genesis 17King James Version (KJV)
17 And when Abram was ninety years old and nine, the Lord appeared to Abram, and said unto him, I am the Almighty God; walk before me, and be thou perfect.
2 And I will make my covenant between me and thee, and will multiply thee exceedingly.
3 And Abram fell on his face:

Sarai laughed when Abram gave her the good news since she believed she was too old to have a child and yet, she *did conceive.* Genesis goes on to add that she'd given birth to a baby named **Isaac;** the infamous son who Abraham nearly killed at Mount Moriah at the behest of the 'Elohim.' Isaac's son, Jacob, went on to father the famous Twelve Patriarchs of the Twelve Tribes of Israel. The *evil ones* from the *Twelve Tribes of Israel* then, subversively, took over the entire world.

9. God vs 'The Gods'

While doing research for this book, as I was reading The Bible all the way through this last time, I made a mysterious observation. I discovered that a Hebrew word chosen to mean *God*—'Elohim'—translates to: 'The Gods'—*not* always '*YHWH,' or 'God,' in singular sense* as we have always been taught. I know that this sounds crazy but, this singular-God semantic-switcheroo is a teaching which has trickled down through theological institutions, beginning at the Ivy League schools, and it came from Jewish scholars predating that.

I believe that these institutions may have wrongfully led the world to believe that Elohim *always* means YHWH, when it *may not in every case*. However, it is important that we don't use this fun Bible study tool as a baseline, since it appears that the word Elohim may have been molested to mean both, 'the gods,' *and,* YHWH—the *Living God* of the Old Testament. It appears that this little tweak *could* be the origin of some of the confusion concerning YHWH's reputation of being a murderous god who demands human sacrifice, which couldn't be further from the truth.

Below, the Hebrew word translated to 'God' is, 'Elohim.' Right after eating of the 'fruit of the tree of the knowledge of good and evil,' in the Adam and

Eve account, we see that *multiple* 'gods' take notice of the shameful fate of the very first human beings, in Genesis 3:22 :

> 'And the LORD God [think of 'God' as '*the* **gods**' here—Hebrew word, '**Elohim**'] said, Behold, the man is become as one of **us**, to know good and evil: and now, lest he put forth his hand, and take also of the tree of life, and eat, and live forever'

It was always hard for me to understand this whole 'one of us' part, since, one thing that the 'Hebrews' have *always* been credited with was the 'invention' of 'monotheism.' Which begs the question: If the Hebrews *were* the 'first' people to believe in 'one God,' then why are we already reading the first book of the Hebrew Bible using a 'polytheistic' narrative? Does The Bible teach of multiple 'gods'? For me there were questions, straightaway, with this translation, since the *very first* of the Ten Commandments says, 'You shall have no other **gods** before me.'

Fallen angels—what we now call 'demons'—were also referred to as 'the gods' in The Bible—it was the exact same word: *Elohim*. Are these two words the same? *They don't seem very interchangeable*; more than that, it's the ultimate paradox: *Good,* and *Evil.* But regardless, *undoubtedly*, in Hebrew, *Elohim* translates to 'the gods' and not simply 'God' as the singular word 'El'—the base word of 'Elohim'—implies; this is the academic excuse for this confusion; they are two different things, however.

If you aren't already sold on this whole 'God vs the gods' theory, perhaps the following verse in Jeremiah will shed some light on this topic for us, in which YHWH *himself* refers to other 'gods' as Elohim, in Jeremiah 7 :

> Jeremiah 7:18 King James Version (KJV)
> **18** The children gather wood, and the fathers kindle the fire, and the women knead their dough, to make cakes to the queen of heaven [Babylonian goddess Ashtaroth], and to pour out drink offerings unto *other gods* [Hebrew word: Elohim], that they may provoke me to anger.

As you probably already know, these 'fallen angels' *aren't* really 'gods' ; this mistranslation was most likely perpetrated, intentionally, by the guilty parties of an age-old tradition of elevating *themselves* to the status of *these* so called 'gods'—those who believe they are the 'offspring' of 'gods.' Perhaps these Biblical accounts have been *mis*-translated by the sons of darkness, to shine an *evil* light on the good, Hebrew, 'Living God' of the Old Testament. And though the word Elohim implies multiple 'gods,' make no mistake that there is only *one true God*.

10. Killing Kids

My first clue to the discovery of this whole God vs 'The Gods' conundrum—the main key, I believe—was hidden in the Isaac and Abraham account. It's the account in which we are told, 'God tempted Abraham' to 'sacrifice his only son, Isaac' on Mount Moriah. Isaac's, is another Bible 'Story' where the word 'Elohim'—'the gods'—is used in place of the word YHWH, or 'God.' But, in which case, something truly remarkable happens: At the end of the account—at the very moment Abraham is about to please 'Elohim' by cutting his son's throat—an 'Angel' from 'YHWH' appears. This 'Angel' of 'YHWH' exclaims, 'Abraham! Abraham!'

At once, Abraham stops and notices this good 'angel of YHWH' who shouted just in time to save his son Isaac's life. Abraham then notices a ram stuck in some vegetation and sacrifices the Ram instead of the boy. This 'boy' went on to grandfather Twelve boys whose offspring would produce the Twelve Tribes of Israel. We are all now blood relatives to this Biblical figure. That is, *if* you believe in The Bible, which, if you don't, you soon will.

Had the fallen angels succeeded in 'tempting' Abraham into dispatching his only son, Isaac, none of us would genetically exist today! At the end of this account, YHWH is applied yet another new name by Abraham: 'Jehovah-jireh' (provider), for 'providing' the ram for sacrifice in place of the boy. Therefore, saving all of our lives. There are clear parallels to the Yeshua account; it was like man's warning from God; a sort of compromise before sin came to the extremes of Christ's sacrifice. Perhaps the 'extremes' of the day were even why God had allowed the Semitic tribes to perform *animal* sacrifice in the first place.

Remember, the Babylonian social climate during Nimrod and Abraham's times was brutal. Once again, just as in the days of the flood of Noah's times, evil had begun to rage. The propaganda and dogma of these creepy societies would have made even a good man prone to evil with the social-programming du jour. If you think this is crazy talk, think about this: We've even seen furnaces, evil and social programming at work, identically, during the last century, when the 'Nazis' turned history back to her dark ways. (**Nazi means 'prince' in Hebrew**.) And, we observed the same in the witch-burnings of Europe before that, and on-and-on prior.

That this 'angel' saved Isaac's life by shouting, means that he had only just entered the scene in this dialogue, so: why would *he* go by the 'angel' of 'YHWH' and only sentences earlier God is supposedly represented by the name 'Elohim,' in the same exact text? Why would the author use two different names for The Living God of The Old Testament, in the same exact story, on the same exact page of The Bible? Perhaps the author uses the absurdity of *a third* name, (*Jehovah-jireh*) being used for the same God *in the same account,* to point to this disparity. It's a clue! No, it's a big, neon sign pointing at the text, saying, 'look,' 'look here,' 'hey you!'

There could be a logical explanation for this: Maybe the first 'god' in the *Isaac human sacrifice story* wasn't God at all but, 'the gods'—*Elohim, demons*—'fallen angels!' Reading the Isaac sacrifice account through this lens brings to life a *Dan-Brownian, Angels-and-Demons-type,* epic battle of *'good* and *evil!'* Just like the account of *Adam and Eve*, itself!

Now God *isn't* this big, bad, monster that the soul-sucking academics have made him out to be. It is their precious satan who is the villain again. Regardless of interpretation, in the end, YHWH *did* intend for Abraham to be tested and as a reward for passing that test, He blessed Abraham's family with Twelve Tribes who would go on to rule the entire world.

The semantics surrounding these events are fun to contemplate but I think that the importance of these accounts always comes into focus when zooming out and *re-*focusing on the *action* of the two forces at work, so not to get bogged down in the quagmire of conjecture. In the Abraham and Isaac account, it is clear that a dark force played a heavy part. Sacrificing one's first born child is an ancient canaanite ritual, and the provision of a ram for sacrifice instead of the boy shows that YHWH was attempting to make a point here: *DON'T MURDER YOUR CHILDREN!*

11. Sacrifice

To this day, there are many sects of 'Jews' who study the ancient '**Babylonian Talmud**,' **which instructs man to sacrifice children to an Old Testament demon named** '**Moloch,**' or 'Molech,' among other spellings. Moloch is the same Demon—'god'—to whom the Twelve Tribes were sacrificing their babies in the Ten Commandments account in which Aaron built the 'golden calf' (the idol of this 'god').

The **Hebrew** word * *Holocaust* means 'sacred cause' and was used by the ancient Canaanites as a word with which to describe their ritual of a *single* human sacrifice. It didn't come to mean 'genocide' until after WWII, when its meaning was changed in dictionaries to reflect the dogma of the day: mass killing of a particular people. The word *holocaust* has even evolved to define a 'cataclysm' ; below under definition 1. *And*, surprisingly, google definition has even brought back an evolution of the word's historic definition, below, under definition 2 :

noun
1. destruction or slaughter on a mass scale, especially caused by fire or nuclear war. "a nuclear holocaust" synonyms: cataclysm, disaster, catastrophe

2. historical : a Jewish sacrificial offering that is burned completely on an altar.

Though, google left out the whole 'human' part.

Even our presidents are cashing in on the ancient Hebrew, Moloch ritual. There is an account found in Hillary Clinton's email leaks which points to an animal sacrifice to *Moloch!* Look at this excerpt from email number 30489 of the WikiLeaks archive. The email is **from Hillary Clinton** to Huma Abedin. Enjoy :

> 'With fingers crossed, the old rabbit's foot out of the box in the attic, **I will be sacrificing a chicken in the backyard to Moloch.**'

You may be saying to yourself, 'oh Hillary's obviously kidding here.' Mmm...*maybe not!* In his memoir *My Life*, former president Bill Clinton romantically scribed a similar account. It was the couple's first trip to Haiti in 1975. The quotes in my edited narrative below are 'Bill's' personal account of the 'most interesting day of the trip' :

> Bill, Hillary and Edwards—the fellow who funded this trip—got a chance to see voodoo in practice in a village near Port-au-Prince. First there was a 'brief course in voodoo theology.' And then the late-afternoon ceremony began. Clinton wrote:

> 'After several minutes of rhythmic dancing to pounding drums, the spirits arrived, seizing a woman and a man. The man proceeded to

rub a burning torch all over his body and walk on hot coals without being burned. The woman, in a frenzy, screamed repeatedly, then grabbed a live chicken and bit its head off. Then the spirits left and those who had been possessed fell to the ground.'

In *My Life*, Bill Clinton went on to document that **his 'brief foray into the world of voodoo' lent to him a special interest in 'the way different cultures try to make sense of life, nature, and the virtually universal belief that there is a nonphysical spirit force at work in the world.**'

The type of sacrificial ritual described in *Hillary's* email is very consistent with those in the 'voodoo' culture of Haiti. Perhaps the above account also inspired Hillary's apparent fascination with animal sacrifice and speaking to 'the gods.'

Animal sacrifice seems a bit uncomfortable to us today—okay, *most* of us—but if God *did* permit it in the Old Testament, it is really something that we ***shouldn't*** concern ourselves with. Yeshua **was the sacrifice to end all sacrifices**, regardless of any Old Testament practices.

12. Tower to 'the gods'

Isaac's son 'Jacob' was the guy who'd had the 'Jacob's ladder' dream. *Jack's*, was another creepy story which never felt right, the method by which he stole his brother's birthright, for one; but there were far too many sketchy events to name so I will leave much of this account to your own research.

Today we will be studying his famous 'Jacob's Ladder' dream which featured 'angels' who made their way in and out of our world **by traveling up and down Jacob's**, '***stairway to heaven.***' In which, the word 'Ladder' was another mistranslation of The Bible. In fact, the Hebrew word the translator has chosen to mean 'ladder' better translates to 'ramp,' or 'steps'—just as the word 'tower' in Nimrod's Tower of Babel story better translates to, 'pyramid.' But Jacob's 'ladder' wasn't a ladder at all! *Again*, it was a pyramid! And a verse in Genesis Chapter 28 emblazons this statement :

> King James Version (KJV)
> [12] And he dreamed, and behold a ladder set up on the earth, **and the top of it reached to heaven**: and behold the angels of God ascending and descending on it.

The statement in the scripture above—**and the top of it reached to heaven in Genesis 28:12**—corresponds perfectly with the following scripture back in Genesis 11, from Nimrod's pyramid account :

> 4 And they said, Go to, let us build us a city and a tower, **whose top may reach unto heaven**; and let us make us a name, lest we be scattered abroad upon the face of the whole earth.

So now this 'Jacob's Ladder' account is *terribly* important since it shamelessly points back to this ancient, spiritual, pyramid technology. And this story tells us *exactly* what this *pyramid* technology was designed to be used for: communicating with 'the gods'—*fallen angels*. In scripture, the name of the location of Jacob's famous nap was changed from *Luz*, to *Bethel* in Genesis 28 :

> King James Version (KJV)
> 18 And Jacob rose up early in the morning, and took the stone that he had put for his pillows, and set it up for a pillar, and poured oil upon the top of it.
> 19 **And he called the name of that place Bethel: but the name of that city was called Luz at the first.**

The original name for this location, *Luz*, means 'Light,' but was thenceforth referred to as *Bethel,* 'house of god,' by Jacob. This means that Jacob's dream about a pyramid, which can be used to communicate with the fallen angels or 'gods,' had occurred in a place which first meant 'light' (a word which doubles as the name of Lucifer—the '*bringer* of light'), after which Jacob renamed the place *Bethel*, which doubles as the word 'god.' Could this fact be a glaring neon sign pointing to the fact that Jacob was made a 'god,' by the 'bringer of light?' This fact shows striking similarities to the pyramid imagery on our one dollar bill, whose capstone emits these rays of 'light.' The title and cover of a book of freemasonry, titled, *A Bridge to Light,* also substantiates this claim. As you know, our one dollar bill too seems to mirror the imagery in Genesis 28:12-13. I implore you to decode the symbolism on our one dollar bill—of an eye, emitting rays of light, hovering above a pyramid—using these two scriptures.

Verse 18 states, '18 And Jacob rose up early in the morning, and took the stone that he had put for his pillows, and set it up for a **pillar**, and poured oil upon the top of it' ; this scripture marks an architectural nexus from which the ancient world made a shift from worshipping demons at pyramid-shaped temples in ancient Egypt to the *Doric* style of building with '**pillars**,' which was exactly what Jacob did: 'set it [the stone] up for a *pillar.*

This 'nexus,' which was clearly inspired by this single Biblical account, actually disguised the old temples—*pyramids*—which had no doubt been connected to evil by the people, during the event horizon of that system of antichrist. The 'pillar'—or 'column'—style of building *hid* this evil pyramid style of temple-building in plain site, since, as with the Parthenon dedicated to Athena in ancient Greece, *these columns actually **elevated** and supported the shape of a pyramid—a triangle*. In Nashville, a full-scale version of the Parthenon has been rebuilt; we will use this structure to demonstrate this architectural evolution from Egyptian to Roman architecture. If you google image the *Nashville Parthenon*, look for the pyramid—*triangle*—which is to this day supported by 'Jacob's Pillars.'

Jacob's architectural 'pillar' element evolved through Greek and Roman times into an architectural 'order' whose components, the *Doric, Ionic,* and later Corinthian, Orders were key steps toward the evolution of our modern skyscrapers. In other words, the pillar was the basic unit of intellectual currency which had led to the construction of the skyscraper, since it had allowed man to build Nimrod's ancient version of the pyramid higher-and-higher. This notion is completely solidified when you study the purpose of each of these 'orders' of architecture since: the *Doric* order referred to the order of the ground floor, then later in time the *Ionic* order was used for the middle story, after which the *Corinthian* or the *Composite Order* was used for the top story.

The *Colossal Order*—the word 'colossal' being late Middle English: via Latin from Greek kolossos **which was applied by Herodotus to the statues of Egyptian temples**—was invented by architects in the Renaissance period. Gustav Eiffel's invention of a steel-framed tower was the next major nexus in this evil evolution of the 'high places' which had originated in the ancient world. The pillars of freemasonry represent this same continuing ascent of Nimrod's Tower into the heavens. The tiered wedding cake also represents man's commitment to this order. And, in the same way, the **'pillar'** on your bed elevates your head every night, which is precisely how *it* came to be known as a, *'**pillow**!' It was named after Jacob's Pillar!*

It is in this blinding light that Jacob's dream appears as some sort of, spiritual star-gate, at which a set of evil instructions were handed to mankind, foretelling a need to evolve the Babylonian system of one world dictatorial government into our modern times, disguised as 'democracy and freedom.' And what a more fitting metaphor could the ancients have chosen, than to incorporate Nimrod's ever-ascending tower into the architectural narrative of this story which, now bridges the oldest of known times to our own in the history of man.

This also explains why Pythagoras—the supposed inventor of the *Pythagorean Theorem of finding the area of a triangle*—is literally worshipped by modern academia. *Pythagoras,* was one of an untold chain of alchemists who have followed Nimrod's ancient plans to march forward into our times. At our end of which, *NASA* has truly 'reached unto heaven.' It is now clear that the 'Elohim'—the fallen angels—*were* the beings who were worshipped on 'Jacob's Ladder.'

In the past, the temples themselves were worshipped as if they were gods; and perhaps the mathematics and knowledge hidden within the architecture itself explains this phenomenon. Consequently, these old sites became academic catchalls from which adventurers could glean knowledge from the past. Rosslyn Chapel, in Scotland, became one such 'catchall' which has been associated with the Knights Templar. The basic building block for the religion of constructing great buildings is the satanic reverence for shapes, numbers and symbolism called, *sacred geometry*. Online, a video, titled, *Donald in Mathmagic Land*, can be found; in which Donald Duck and his 'spirit guide' explain to children the meaning behind sacred geometry and how it applies to art, architecture, technology, and mathematics.

When watching this crazy video, notice Disney paying homage to Pythagoras worship, a pyramid held up by Jacob's Pillars (the Parthenon), the 'golden rectangles' in their new temple (the United Nations building), the wreath of Apollo upon Donald's head, and the pentagram on his hand which is, as Donald's spirit guide explains, the mathematical foundation upon which all ancient *and modern* buildings were built. Also, Keep your eyes peeled for the many other layers of grim symbolism being taught to our children.

Scriptural 'Tweaks'

The aforementioned word *Elohim,* which was tweaked to mean *'God,'* mandates the belief that either The Bible is *polytheistic* or that, The Hebrew God of the Pentateuch, suggested, condoned, and 'tempted' people to commit human sacrifice—an 'abomination' for which the warring Hebrews (God's 'chosen people') extinguished all of those tribes of babykillers in the Old Testament. These 'baby-killers' *made* their sacrifices at these 'high places,' or, 'pyramids.' Many of these 'extinguished tribes' were 'giants' or 'Nephilim,' including Goliath of the epic David and Goliath account of a Hebrew beheading a Philistine 'giant.' One said tribe of 'giants' which the Twelve Hebrew Tribes defeated referred to themselves as

'*Moabites,*' after which the *MOAB*—the supposed, **Mother Off All Bombs** —was named.

Today, people from the same tribe as Goliath, from the *David and Goliath* account, now refer to themselves as '*Palestinians.*' Once again we see the 'Philistines' in the news in our day, for their demonstrations against a modern-day pyramid-builder—Trump's—recent announcement to move 'Israel's' Capitol to Jerusalem, along with the US embassy; this socially disruptive action will once again incite a horrible uprising which *will*, eventually, result in Armageddon—*the war to end all wars*—this horrible event will begin in Jerusalem and spread outward in all directions (Zechariah 14:2).

If you study how the prophecies of the Abrahamic religions intertwine, you will immediately realize the powerful social programming which will lead to the State of Israel (the 'Jews') and Palestine (the Muslims) squaring off in this epic battle of the ages. Ironically, many Muslims *despise* 'Jews,' not realizing that they **are**, themselves, 'Hebrews' if they truly believe their own Quran. The three Pentateuch-reading religions—*Judaism*, *Islam*, and *Christianity*—are referred to as the 'Abrahamic' religions. What separates the three is, the 'denial' of Christ being our 'Lord and Savior'—*the ancient mechanism of antichrist*. If you will remember, this was one of the central requirements for partaking in the 'Knowledge of Good and Evil' : 'the denial of the existence of God.' Most readers never catch on to any of these scriptural nuances, ('tweaks') and head to their respective temples every week simply to play church.

You may be questioning God's tolerance of this ambiguity within the Scriptures but, these tweaks—*which have been edited into the Good and Evil theme of The Bible*—have allowed The Bible to remain in print for all of these years. If these Biblical accounts had been made as clear as we are making them today, The Bible would've disrupted this evil system which has allowed men to become 'gods' for so long, therefore forcing our demise long ago. This is an obvious cover-up which was perpetrated by the guardians of the Biblical 'canon.'

Here, I will pose to you a few questions:

1. What if the Biblical Tower of Babel account had used the word 'pyramid' instead of the chosen mistranslation?
2. If so, would you not more easily connect the dots to this age old scam?
3. What if the Jacob's Ladder story had clearly stated that these fallen angels—*Elohim*—had been using a pyramid to travel freely between our world and their 'first estate?'

The slight nuances in the translation of the Holy Text were a major victory for the sons of darkness who've been doling out our knowledge and technology since ancient times. These minor 'tweaks,' which leave the user looking solely for the meaning hidden in individual Biblical accounts, discourage the reader from threading these accounts into 'one Bible Story.' The keepers of knowledge even outlawed ownership of The Bible for we commoners, or 'vulgar,' for most of its existence. This is how the first Greek translation of The Bible earned its name, 'the Vulgate.' Because it was *re*-edited for the 'vulgar,' also known as, *'commoners.'* These 'tweaks' have lent a major element of ambiguity to the scriptures for people who simply occasionally read but don't study the Bible—which disturbingly, *is most of us*.

True Christianity in Christ's and his apostles' times, as it still is today, has always been highly frowned upon in its purest form. This is why Yeshua and his apostles were always on the run in the gospels, and nearly every one of them were crucified and put to death, *just as was Christ*. One way that you will *know* when you have become a true member of this *most-secret society* is, you will begin to feel the world breathing down your neck; you will encroach that danger zone where your beliefs begin to threaten the system of antichrist which allows the man of lawlessness to maintain his throne. This 'system of antichrist' includes most of today's churches and their teachings. Eventually the teachings of Christianity themselves will become a 'terrorist activity' and the man or woman perpetrating such an act will be put to death—this is confirmed in Revelation.

13. Twelve Tribes

Up to this point in our travels: we have witnessed creation, creation of man and our fall from YHWH, Noah's Ark which saved all of mankind after they became wicked and YHWH flooded the world, King Nimrod's horrible conquest and his invention of the pyramid of oppression, Abraham's covenant with YHWH, the account in which Abraham nearly killed Isaac, and we learned the account of Jacob's ladder. *Now*, on with our epic:

Abraham begat Isaac and Isaac's son *Jacob* begat Twelve incredibly famous sons: Reuben, Simeon, Levi, **Judah**, Dan, Naphtali, Gad, Asher, Issachar, Zebulun, Joseph, and Benjamin. From these Twelve Tribes would come the 'Children of Israel.' (It is a shame to whiz by the many wonderful accounts that we are forced to miss during this study but that will leave a lifetime of adventure for you the reader long after you and I are forced to make our separate ways.)

The 'Story' of these Twelve Tribes, if I had to sum them up in a sentence, would be: 'Twelve Hebrew Tribes of slaves who freed themselves, became great warriors, and conquered the entire world.' It really is an incredible account and when you soon realize that the same Hebrew Tribes are seated at all of the thrones on earth, it will change something inside of you; the 'stories' in the black book holding your door open will become a virtual wonderland of information— *The Living Word!*

The *Cohens* | Origins of Democracy

The origins of democracy and social organization are hidden in plain sight within The Bible's text. These Hebrew warriors were a nomadic group therefore every belonging the Hebrew Tribes owned was mobile. Since the Israelites had become nomadic, these great tribes learned to organize like man had never seen before.

YHWH issued every Tribe a purpose in the community, for example: The Levites were appointed as the Priests and they became responsible for the Ark, the mobile Synagogue and the Priestly Vestments. The 'Priestly Vestments' consisted of the 'Ephod' (Priestly garments) to which the Holy Grail, *the Holy Breastplate*, was attached; this was the Templar's primary object of interest (I provide much more detail on this topic in my Amazon #1 Bestseller *Sacred Scroll of Seven Seals)*. The Hebrew High Priest, in old times, was known as a 'Cohen.'

The *Cohen* settled any and all disputes among the group; he was the highest judge in the land which is why the Holy Grail, which this High Priest wore on his chest, is also referred to as the 'Breastplate of **Judgment**.' We can still observe the residue of the Tribe of Levi within the etymology of the following English words which pertain to the resolution of disputes, still today; all of these words were derived from the word Judah (JEW): Judge, Jurisprudence, Jury, and Justice.

Even in our own times we see law firms identified with names such as 'Cohen and Cohen.' The field of law is strewn from one end to the other with men and women having semitic forms of this name along with many others which are similar, and they all stem from this Tribe of Hebrew warriors who all began with Abraham, Isaac, Jacob, and Jacob's Twelve Sons. This is where the famous term of endearment 'God of Abraham, Isaac and Jacob,' was derived. There are at least 42 verses in the KJV of The Bible where God is known by this term. Acts 7 :

> King James Version (KJV)
> **32** Saying, **I am the God of thy fathers, the God of Abraham, and the God of Isaac, and the God of Jacob**. Then Moses trembled, and durst not behold.

The High Priesthood represented the man who ruled over the entire world for these Semitic Tribes.

The Holy Grail
As aforementioned, the Holy Grail is a braided gold chest plate, worn by the Hebrew High Priest, to which Twelve **jew**els were attached; the name of each individual Tribe was scribed upon each of these Twelve **jew**els to represent that Tribe. (Even the *word* **Jew**el is a Hebrew form of the word '**Jew**'—what a perfect symbol for the jews attachment to YHWH through The High Priesthood.)

The 'Breastplate of Judgment' was used for speaking to God via the *'Urim* and *Thummim'* ; *two rocks - one black, one white, were attached to the*

Holy Grail and used something like dice. For example: At random, the High Priest would choose a stone, then, based on the color drawn, the High Priest would repeatedly split the people into two groups to reveal which group contained the guilty party, or, the 'sinner.' As the account records, eventually, the Holy Grail was used to communicate directly with *satan* himself; at this time, sadly, the evil ones had begun using the Grail, *exclusively*, for divination.

The Bible tells us that the Breastplate of Judgment was involved in all aspects of living. Through these Priestly Vestments, YHWH instructed the Prophets and kings in matters concerning law, punishments, architecture, and even war. The Israelites employed the Breastplate considerably while cleansing the land of Canaan of the tribes of baby-killers and 'giants' who had, once again, threatened the very existence of humanity.

The Holy Grail wandered in the wilderness worn by Aaron, with Moses and the Twelve Tribes. Satirically, the Grail was later strapped around the neck of 'Caiaphas,' the wicked High Priest and leader of the 'Jewish' Sanhedrin, when he played a lead role in the brutal crucifixion of Yeshua; the fact that the highest Judge in the land wore this gold and jewel-encrusted treasure when perpetrating the greatest single tragedy in human history lends the already coveted Grail a dark power which has left many a satanic Knight defenseless to the seduction of this bastardized Holy relic.

This Holy Relic was even *called* the *'Holy'* Breastplate! *And*, the French word for **'plate'** during the times in which the *Grail* legend originated was, astonishingly: **'*Grail!*'** 'Grail' didn't come to mean 'cup' until centuries later!

So, in other words, 'Holy Grail' WAS the Biblical name for the 'Breast-**plate** of Judgment!' Yeshua's cup *wasn't* called the 'Holy' *cup* so, why would an unrecognizable drinking vessel become an object of interest? It just doesn't add up and, again, if you read the **SSOSS**, things will become crystal clear for you. In order to cover their tracks and to thin any competition to the High Priesthood and possession of what had become their most precious idol, the sons of darkness invented Arthurian literature which has now left the entire world looking for a silly cup.

Upon threat of siege on Jerusalem, the Grail was placed in hiding, most likely buried under the Temple of Solomon over which the 'High Priest' presided. The Grail then became the object of interest for holders of sacred knowledge, around the world, for millennia. The most successful of which were the infamous nine knights—the 'Knights Templar'—who traveled **2,800 miles** *all the way from France* in order to take back what they believed had rightfully belonged to them—the High Priesthood. But, why? There is only one reason for this: These nine men were hiding an amazing secret! That is, they, *themselves*, are **Jews**! Though they desperately hid their Jewish heritage to protect their dirty little scam.

How about this: After the Knights Templar sieged Jerusalem, and setup shop *on* the Temple site, they even *named themselves after the Temple of Solomon: The Poor Fellow-Soldiers of Christ and of the* **Temple of Solomon** (Latin: *Pauperes commilitones Christi* **Templique Salomonici**). The Templar were also known simply as the *Order of* **Solomon's Temple**. *Since their very name shamelessly exploits the name of this Jewish Holy Site*, the Gold and jewel-encrusted *Breastplate of Judgment—which was* *worn by the High Priest over the Temple—is certainly the greatest Holy Treasure one in their Order could possess. Does it not seem so obvious now?*

The greatest irony in all of this is the unbelievable fact that adventure seekers have exhausted great fortunes hunting for this elusive object, literary scholars have spent incalculable lifetimes with their noses buried in codex after codex searching for clues to the identity of this old thing and, all the while, the entire account of its making and journey have been brilliantly recorded in the most widely published and distributed account in human history—*the Holy Bible*. The account of the construction of the Breastplate of Judgment—and the *ephod*—is even longer than that of the account of The Tower of Babel.

The Ark

The Ark of the Covenant, also known as the Ark of the Testimony, is a gold-gilded, rectangular, wooden chest with a lid covering. Adorning the lid were two golden Cherubim facing each other and their wings were pointed forward toward one another. The Ark was described in the Book of Exodus and was said to contain the two stone tablets of the Ten Commandments along with Aaron's rod and a pot of manna (the bread-like substance which YHWH provided the Israelites for food when they wandered in the wilderness for all of those years). *Our English word exit, which means, 'an act of going out of or leaving a place,' was derived from the Hebrew word 'Exodus.'*

After the Hebrews *left* Egypt, the 'Ark,' which was said to contain the power of YHWH himself, was carried around the wilderness with the Twelve Tribes, until Solomon, the third King of Judah placed the Ark in the 'Synagogue' (Holy of Holies') of the first Temple. The 'Synagogue' was nothing more than a tent for the forty years that these Tribes remained 'nomadic' in the 'wilderness.'

The Ark was incredibly powerful and couldn't even be physically touched since doing so was known to strike man dead, *on the spot*. 2 Samuel 6 :

> King James Version (KJV)
> **6** And when they came to Nachon's threshingfloor, **Uzzah** put forth his hand to the ark of God, and took hold of it; for the oxen shook it.
> **7** And the anger of the Lord was kindled against **Uzzah; and God smote him** there for his error; and there he died by the ark of God.

The *Uzi* submachine gun was supposedly designed and named after Captain *Uziel* Gal of the *Israel* Defense Forces (IDF) **following the 1948 Arab-Israeli War**. We can be fairly certain that this **Captain *'Uziel'*** guy was simply given credit for sharing a form of the same name with a guy who touched another weapon which struck men dead: **Uzzah**, *who died after touching the Ark of the Covenant*.

The 'Cohen'—*Priest*—was the *only* man who could enter the Synagogue without being struck dead by YHWH; if you will recall, *the Cohen was the man with the Holy Grail strapped around his neck*. A rope was tied to the Priest's foot by which he could be pulled from the room of the Holy of

Holies, were he struck dead while performing his Priestly duties, which is precisely how the sons of *Aaron*—the very first Hebrew High Priest—died after 'offering strange fire'—*fascinating!* Leviticus 10 :

> **10** And Nadab and Abihu, **the sons of Aaron**, took either of them his censer, and put fire therein, and put incense thereon, and **offered strange fire before the Lord**, which he commanded them not.

The central feature of the Holy of Holies, the *Ark of the Covenant* was even famously featured in the George Lucas film, *Raiders of the Lost* **Ark**. Lucas himself is openly semitic and judging from his films he has an ***extensive*** understanding of the 'Dark Side.' It is ironic that Lucas would make a feature blockbuster film based on this semitic treasure which was 'lost' in the folds of history years ago. This is a Jewish treasure which had been glorified by Hollywood and no one even twitched an eyebrow.

It is also a point of great satire that Lucas shone attention upon the object which stood *right beside the actual Holy Grail*— **The Holy Breastplate**.

14. Pillars of Cloud and Fire

The offspring of the Twelve Sons of Jacob—*The Twelve Tribes*—had become enslaved by the same system of antichrist as we've discussed. They'd become **masons** in Egypt who were building the many great structures of their time. Moses and his older brother Aaron came together before the Pharaoh and after a series of truly miraculous events, Pharaoh *'let his people go.'*

Moses and Aaron then led this group through the wilderness for forty years. They nomadically moved from place to place while looking for the land that YHWH had promised them—'***The Promised Land.***' God would've simply led His people directly toward their *inheritance* (*promised land*), had they not spent the whole time grumbling about their conditions. They grew tired of the 'manna' YHWH had provided them to eat and so-on and so-forth; they were *bitter* people.

God was even *living amongst these people*, appearing to them as a 'pillar of cloud' by day and a 'pillar of fire' by night to guide their way. At the US capitol building, a masonic representation of these two pillars stands to each side of the speaker's podium which represents the same dumb, old game: becoming god!

God was even *living amongst these people*, appearing to them as a 'pillar of cloud' by day and a 'pillar of fire' by night to guide their way. King Solomon's Temple incorporated the symbolism of these two 'pillars' which had also held up the front porch of the Temple, which is a haunting reminder of the symbolism in the previous account of *Jacob's* **Pillar**'; many groups, including the freemasons, began to simply worship these *pillars* in an act known in their own literature as, *'pillar worship.'* At the US capitol building, a masonic representation of these two pillars stands to each side of the speaker's podium which represents the same dumb, old game: *becoming your 'god!'*

Even *numbering people* began with this group; it was called the census and YHWH did *not* like it! I Chronicles states that satan provoked David to 'number' his people for which 'God smote Israel.' Even numbering men for the purpose of war was abominable in the eyes of YHWH since it showed a lack of trust in Him.

The Israelites physically witnessed miracle after miracle worked by their God but still weren't satisfied, and many even wished they'd have just stayed in Egypt where at least they'd had what they were accustomed to eating as *food and permanent shelter* (in Egypt, these people must have been enslaved similarly to us).

The laws being imposed on the Tribes began to stack up. There was a law for nearly everything, just like we have today. The peoples' bickering had also grown to an uproar at which time Moses went atop Mount Sinai and YHWH carved those famous Ten Rules upon those two stone tablets.

*Now....*God has been given a bad rap for over-imposing restrictions upon us, but, the Ten Commandments account shows that this couldn't be further from being true.

This old trick of tightening the bindings of enslavement through the excessive enforcement of law has its roots in ancient Babylon, look: In October 1977, the Government of Iraq—*the home of ancient Babylon*—presented a replica of the original stele enumerating the Babylonian laws of Hammurabi to the United Nations in New York City—*the world headquarters of New Babylon*—the oldest written code of laws known to mankind. The stele depicts Hammurabi facing the God of the Sun and receiving the Code of Laws from him. There are many ancient Babylonian artifacts strewn about the UN, most of which were organized in cooperation with Yale University. The game which Aaron, the High Priest of the Israelites, was running seems to be a timeworn technology of slavery.

There were many different strange factors at play in this account. But, again, if you break it down to the major forces at work, here, you have a group of complainers in the valley below who built a 'golden calf' statue to 'Moloch,' after which they built a fire in which they began to toss their babies, *after being smothered by rules*. And at the top of the mountain you have Moses who was righteous in the eyes of YHWH, who was receiving just Ten simple Rules to follow.

This 'zoomed-out' view shows that man had been imposing heaps of laws on the Israelites that couldn't possibly have been obeyed, and YHWH was shouting: 'ENOUGH!' ENOUGH! This explains the new name that YHWH had given Jacob all those years ago: 'Israel,' meaning 'God contended.' This name is very fitting considering the fact that YHWH was constantly *'struggling' to keep his people from burning their own babies alive.*

15. First King of Judah

Though the order with which YHWH structured the Israelites birthed the very first democratic society, these people would never quite get it right; they begged YHWH to give them a leader so that they could have a powerful king over them like other nations. I Samuel 8 :

King James Version (KJV)

5 And [The Children of Israel] said unto him [Samuel the Prophet], Behold, thou art old, and thy sons walk not in thy ways: now **make us a king to judge us like all the nations**.

6 But the thing displeased Samuel, when **they said, Give us a king to judge us**. And Samuel prayed unto the Lord.

7 And **the Lord said unto Samuel**, Hearken unto the voice of the people in all that they say unto thee: for they have not rejected thee, but **they have rejected me, that I should not reign over them**.

8 According to all the works which they have done since the day that **I brought them up out of Egypt** even unto this day, wherewith **they have forsaken me, and served other *gods***, so do they also unto thee.

9 Now therefore hearken unto their voice: howbeit yet protest solemnly unto them, and **shew them the manner of the king that shall reign over them**.

10 And Samuel told all the words of the Lord unto the people that asked of him a king.

11 And he said, **This will be the manner of the king that shall reign over you: He will take your sons, and appoint them for himself, for his chariots, and to be his horsemen; and some shall run before his chariots**.

12 And he will appoint him captains over thousands, and captains over fifties; and will set them to ear his ground, **and to reap his harvest, and to make his instruments of war**, and instruments of his chariots.

13 And **he will take your daughters to be confectionaries, and to be cooks, and to be bakers**.

14 And **he will take your fields, and your vineyards, and your oliveyards, even the best of them, and give them to his servants**.

15 And **he will take the tenth of your seed, and of your vineyards, and give to his officers, and to his servants**.

16 And he will take your menservants, and your maidservants, and your goodliest young men, and your asses, and put them to his work.

17 He will take the tenth of your sheep: and ye shall be his servants.

18 And ye shall cry out in that day because of your king which ye shall have chosen you; and **the Lord will not hear you in that day**.
19 Nevertheless **the people refused to obey the voice of Samuel**; and **they said**, Nay; **but we will have a king over us**;
20 That we also may be like all the nations; and **that our king may judge us**, and go out before us, and fight our battles.
21 And Samuel heard all the words of the people, and he rehearsed them in the ears of the Lord.
22 And the Lord said to Samuel, Hearken unto their voice, and make them a king. And Samuel said unto the men of Israel, Go ye every man unto his city.

This was the beginning of the woes we see today.

YHWH clearly didn't want this for His people so he fought them ruggedly, finally caving in, at which point they found King Saul—*the first King of Judah*—to fulfill YHWH's famous covenant with Abraham which stated that, Abraham's seed would be the Kings of all nations. The crowning of King Saul would be the genesis of a horrible reign of terror for most of the rest of Judah's existence, *including those of Us today.*

Saul was, himself, a 'giant.' Look, 1 Samuel 9 :

> King James Version (KJV)
> **2** And he had a son, whose name was Saul, a choice young man, and a goodly: and there was not among the children of Israel a

goodlier person than he: **from his shoulders and upward he was higher than any of the people**.

Saul may have been 'goodly' but, this passage doesn't imply that Saul was a 'good' man; *goodly means tall, or large!* Here is the account where David, a young shepherd boy, first meets King Saul, the first King of Judah. I Samuel 16 :

King James Version (KJV)
14 But the Spirit of the Lord departed from Saul, and an evil spirit from the Lord troubled him.
15 And Saul's servants said unto him, Behold now, **an evil spirit from God troubleth thee**.
16 Let our lord now command thy servants, which are before thee, to seek out a man, who is a cunning player on an harp: and it shall come to pass, when the evil spirit from God is upon thee, that he shall play with his hand, and thou shalt be well.
17 And Saul said unto his servants, Provide me now a man that can play well, and bring him to me.
18 Then answered one of the servants, and said, Behold, I have seen a son of Jesse the Bethlehemite, that is cunning in playing, and a mighty valiant man, and a man of war, and prudent in matters, and a comely person, and the Lord is with him.
19 Wherefore Saul sent messengers unto Jesse, and said, **Send me David thy son, which is with the sheep**.
20 And Jesse took an ass laden with bread, and a bottle of wine, and a kid, **and sent them by David his son unto Saul**.

21 And David came to Saul, and stood before him: and he loved him greatly; and he became his armourbearer.

So, Saul was a demon-possessed giant, and when David famously played his harp for the King, he would relax. This must have been a brutally-ugly sight to behold but David played for the King to ward off this *evil spirit* when it manifest through Saul.

To make a long story short, David was a handsome young man and a great warrior. As mentioned earlier, he even beheaded a Philistine giant—*Goliath*. David grew fond of Saul's daughter *Michal*. And, this moment marks the point in time at which Saul's dirty bloodline infiltrated the bloodline of David; *the Royal Blood of the Tribe of Judah*. As a challenge—believing there was no way David could pull it off—Saul asked David to kill 100 Philistines and bring back the foreskins of their penises, and only then would he allow David to marry his daughter. Here is what David did…I Samuel 18 :

King James Version (KJV)
27 Wherefore David arose and went, he and his men, and slew of the Philistines **two hundred men**; and **David brought their foreskins, and they gave them in full tale to the king**, that he might be the king's son in law. And Saul gave him Michal his daughter to wife.

The account goes on to say that this wild-eyed, love-drunk warrior actually 'scared' Saul, and this *should've* scared him. The Philistines were some of the most brutal, gigantic, evil warriors who have ever strayed earth, and David was eating them for breakfast, lunch, and *dinner*.

The 'evil spirits' which 'troubled' Saul are still *'troubling'* our leaders today. The fraternity from Yale, *The Order of Skull and Bones*, preserves rituals in which they use the bones of the dead as spiritual conduit in order to pass these same evil spirits from one generation to the next.

Prescott Bush, *Dubya's* granddad is one of a group of Skull and Bones members who robbed the grave of Geronimo and brought his head back to their clubhouse on **High** Street's *The Tomb,* for the same purpose. This isn't a conspiracy 'theory,' it is mentioned in 'The Order's' own 'minutes.' The name 'Geronimo' is *no* indian name, either. It is an English evolution of the name Jehoram which was another wicked King of Judah—the son of the most-wicked, baal-worshiping, idolatrous, *Jezibel*.

I would like to point out that, 'Geronimo'—*Jehoram*—was also Osama bin Laden's code name during 'Operation Neptune,' during which bin Laden was shot and killed (Neptune is another name for Nimrod—in the Atlantis story he built a 'high place'). And, Osama's body was supposedly 'dumped in the ocean.' *Hmmm...*

Would you believe that this ancient Skull and Bones ritual actually *began* with King Saul? Here you go...I Samuel 31 :

King James Version (KJV)

9 And they cut off his head, and stripped off his armour, and sent into the land of the Philistines round about, to publish it in the house of their idols, and among the people.
10 And they put his armour in the house of * Ashtaroth: and they fastened his body to the wall of Bethshan.

> Note: * ***Ashtaroth**—also known as **Ishtar**—is another demonic deity which demands bloody human sacrifice. Ishtar was the 'goddess' of the main gate when entering ancient **Babylon** (more on this soon). Sadly, Ishtar is also the name for which we've named the celebration of the resurrection of Christ: '**Easter**.'*

The Order of Skull and Bones invents and creates our enemies for the purpose of controlled conflict and then harvests the heads of those enemies when their purpose has been fulfilled. It makes one wonder if the above verse is the *origin* of The Order's evil rituals or, is this simply the historical documentation of an ancient evolution of S&B infiltrating the Kings of Judah? I ere on the side that these despotic practices stretch deep into the darkness of unrecorded history and this was all part of a plot to overtake the Hebrew democracy.

The Order of Skull and Bones's logo goes right along with our whole 'playing god' theme, too, since it is inscribed with the numbers 3:22. The origin of the numbers on their logo proudly illustrates to the world that they are 'our gods' and that they have eaten of the 'forbidden fruit' ; it also demonstrates The Order's objective, which is to rob us of the eternal life which

YHWH has promised us. And now, I give you the alarming origin of The Order of Skull and Bones's beloved **3:22** logo....***Genesis**, **3:22*** :

> 'And the LORD God [think of 'God' as '***the** gods*' here—Hebrew word, '**Elohim**'] said, **Behold, the man is become as one of us, to know good and evil: and now, lest he put forth his hand, and take also of the tree of life, and eat, and live forever**'

The Order of Skull and Bones relishes in the fact that they've stolen the High Priesthood of Christ and even *most of our souls!* The Order's disgusting actions are no different from those of Nimrod: they have removed God from our schools by teaching Darwinism and from the ancient Roman satanic bible, which has empowered them to now become our 'gods.' We have woefully fallen head first into an age old scam which has now been galvanized as *science* and *technology*.

The ancient practice of harvesting and communicating with human heads is practiced by the Jesuit Order of the Catholic Church, the vikings and even the Knights Templar. In an operation coined, **Yalegate**, a group of students who are said to have broken-into **The Tomb** on Yale's **High** Street, claim that *Hitler's* silverware—among many other sinister souvenirs *including many, many skulls*—are placed in their temple to satan. Let us not forget that Hitler's body too was never found.

All in all there were a total of 20 Kings of Judah, out of which only 5 were righteous kings: *King Josiah, King Hezekiah, King Jotham, King Jehoshaphat*, and *King Abijah...That's it!* Other than the handful listed above, things pretty much went downhill, *quickly*. Even the good Kings of Judah had so much evil to remove from their kingdoms that cleaning things up must've been an exercise in futility.

The Biblical account reports that *Rehoboam*, in around 930 BC, split the country into two kingdoms: the *Kingdom of Israel*—which included the cities of *Shechem* and *Samaria*—in the north, and the *Kingdom of Judah*—containing *Jerusalem*—in the South. Sadly, Judah had split into these two kingdoms to give way for the same old scam, *controlled conflict*. Even after YHWH had given this group a perfect way to govern themselves in times of peace, *and war*, their arrogance had thrust them right back into the system of *antichrist:* dividing kingdoms and manipulating them against each other in every way possible.

To go along with the whole Royal Family Tribe of Judah theme, guess what the name of the new split kingdom of Judah was called? Time's up: *The United Kingdom!* That's right, they called it the *UK!* You just can't make this stuff up.

Solomon's sins broke his agreement with YHWH and enacted all of the curses applied to Solomon concerning his misuse of the Temple, and it did indeed come by 'the striped backs of his people.' Look again at 2 Samuel 7 :

> King James Version (KJV)

14 I will be his father, and he shall be my son. **If he commit iniquity, I will chasten him with the rod of men, and with the stripes of the children of men**:
15 But my **mercy shall not depart away from him, as I took it from Saul, whom I put away before thee**.

As unbelievable as it may seem, YHWH *did* leave these evil men in charge, due to our ancestors' stiff-necked ignorance. And as you will see in the upcoming chapter in which we chase Prince William's bloodline *all the way back to Adam and Eve*, they are *still* 'in charge.' YHWH removed Saul as the head of His people but, as promised above, he wouldn't do it again. *Incredible!*

16. Temple of Doom

After wandering idly for forty years, the Twelve Tribes finally began to cleanse Canaan of the 'giants' and evil ones who ritually murdered their own children, and immediately began taking their places in the 'Promised Land.' David conquered Jerusalem by defeating the *Jebusites* in 1052 BC —another tribe of 'giants' (note: Jeb is the name to which George Bush's brother answers). 2 Samuel 7 :

> King James Version (KJV)
> **1** And it came to pass, when the king sat in his house, and the Lord had given him rest round about from all his enemies;
> **2** That the king said unto Nathan the prophet, See now, **I dwell in an house of cedar, but the ark of God dwelleth within curtains**.

Since settling down, David had built himself a Palace fit for a king but had had a moment of solace when he realized that he hadn't done the same for YHWH and the mobile synagogue still only amounted to a *tent—'curtains.'* Nathan, David's Prophet, gave his blessing for the construction of the great structure but, The Lord came to Nathan that night and forbade Nathan to allow the structure to be built by David. Below, we will once again view 2 Samuel 7 :

King James Version (KJV)

12 And when thy days be fulfilled, and thou shalt sleep with thy fathers, **I will set up thy seed after thee [Solomon]**, which shall proceed out of thy bowels, and I will establish his kingdom.

13 He shall build an house for my name, and **I will stablish the throne of his kingdom for ever.**

14 I will be his father, and he shall be my son. **If he commit iniquity, I will chasten him with the rod of men, and with the stripes of the children of men**:

15 But my **mercy shall not depart away from him, as I took it from Saul, whom I put away before thee.**

16 And thine house and thy kingdom shall be established for ever before thee: thy throne shall be established for ever.

17 According to all these words, and according to all this vision, so did Nathan speak unto David.

Many think the Temple was a good thing but I beg to differ. When carefully analyzed, YHWH sounded *quite* reluctant about the building of the Temple from the very start; even the *name, Temple of Solomon,* implies that this structure was built for *Solomon, not YHWH*. After all, had it been built for YHWH, wouldn't Solomon have named the structure, *YHWH's Temple?* Verse 12 above states that, Solomon '**shall** built an house in my name,' which doesn't exactly imply that this was God's will. So, *God forbade Solomon's father David from building the Temple,* and commented further that Solomon *would* build it, not necessarily that he, *should*.

We know for a fact that YHWH did *not* want a king (besides Him) to rule over His people; yet, YHWH told David that He *would* establish for David, a 'house, a throne and a kingdom, forever,' in nearly the same breath as he'd reluctantly agreed to the building of the Temple (in verse 13). And I think that, subsequently, the kingship and Temple had become a sort of proving grounds for Judah and their coveted kings: The Temple and kingship had become a 'necessary evil' for this obstacle course known as the 'Valley of the Shadow of Death,' but only after YHWH's people had, repeatedly, badgered YHWH until he finally became wroth at their ignorance.

The fact that the Temple itself *had become an idol,* and a vehicle for man to *elevate himself to god status*—just as with King Nimrod's terrible pyramid—the Temple provided the ultimate examination of a man's heart and intentions; unfortunately most of us fail at that lousy promotion and even take advantage of our power in the *mail room. So*, Solomon's Temple, in all of its Glory after YHWH was added, had become the ultimate booby trap in which King Solomon himself had become ensnared.

Verse 14, *above*, 'I will be his father, and he shall be my son. **If he commit iniquity, I will chasten him with the rod of men, and with the stripes of the children of men**…,' further substantiates our suspicions of YHWH's reluctance to allow the Temple to be built since, **this verse came with a serious threat!**

So, in summary, YHWH had *allowed* the Temple to be built but if Solomon got it wrong, which now we know he got it *seriously wrong*, YHWH would '**chasten him with the stripes of the children of men.**' This time, YHWH implied, He will have '***no mercy***' on His people as He'd had in the case of Saul, but that His '**mercy shall not depart**' from the *subsequent kings of Judah instead.* Wow! *So right here*, before the Temple is even built, YHWH points to the fact that He knew the Temple would be used in ways which would *not* honor Him.

And lastly, the scriptures below demonstrate that YHWH lovingly wished to remain living 'in a tent,' among 'His people.' 2 Samuel 7 :

> **5** Go and tell my servant David, Thus saith the Lord, Shalt thou build me an house for me to dwell in?
> **6** Whereas **I have not dwelt in any house since the time that I brought up the children of Israel out of Egypt,** even to this day, **but have walked in a tent and in a tabernacle.**
> **7** In all the places wherein **I have walked with all the children of Israel spake I a word with any of the tribes of Israel, whom I commanded to feed my people Israel, saying, Why build ye not me an house of cedar**?

The whole 'David' had too much 'blood on his hands' being the *only* reason YHWH wouldn't allow the Temple to be built no longer holds any water since, the final verse above makes it very clear that YHWH loved being with His people.

Still, David purchased the threshing floor owned by Araunah the Jebusite, with the intentions of building YHWH's great Temple. The ominous location chosen for the Temple also happens to be the exact site where Solomon's ancestor Abraham had nearly cut the throat of his son Isaac, at the behest of the *Elohim*—an event which would surely have prevented the Temple from ever having been built in the first place. (According to google, a 'threshing floor separates grain from [a plant], typically with a flail or by the action of a revolving mechanism.')

The Temple is the centerpiece of Islam, Christianity, Judaism, freemasonry and many other religions, cults, and even devil worship. 'Jews' face toward the ancient site of King Solomon's infamous *idol* when they pray, *to this day*—no matter where on earth these followers stand—they *always* turn toward the Temple to pray. The 'Black Stone of Mecca,' or the *Kaaba stone*, is a Muslim relic. The stone, according to Islamic tradition, dates back to the times of Adam and Eve. The black meteorite is the eastern cornerstone of the Kaaba, which is the ancient, sacred, stone building towards which *Muslims also always pray.*

The 'stone building' is said to mimic the dimensions of the 'Holy of Holies,' which is the room in which the Ark was placed inside Solomon's Temple. *So*, to clarify: Muslims built a version of God's room in Solomon's Temple, painted it **black,** and threw a fallen piece of a planet inside the box for the purpose of *worshipping the rock*. The tribes of 'giants' in the Old Testament *also* worshipped the stars, moon, and planets. As earlier noted, horoscopes began in ancient Babylon; and Solomon too is associated with astrology in countless mystical writings.

This means that the site where Solomon's Temple stood *is* the most revered Holy site on earth. The Temple has always been at the center of the whole 'doomsday' conversation too, since Biblical prophecy states that the erection of the third Temple will signal the beginning of the end.

The First Temple was built by Solomon and was destroyed by king Nebuchadnezzar in 586 BC. From 516 BC to 70 AD, The Temple was rebuilt after the Jews returned from Babylonian captivity. King Herod expanded and beautified The Temple to the degree that some even considered the renovations to be the prophetic 'Third Temple.' King Herod was the Jewish-*convert,* ruler of Jerusalem who ultimately ordered the death of Christ. So Herod's heavy involvement in the Temple shows that he was working hand in hand with the Jewish Sanhedrin and they were operating the great Temple like an evil amusement park.

It took 46 years to complete the main Temple and another 36 years to finish the entire Temple complex. This new temple was said to be a larger and more beautiful temple than the one that Solomon had built. The historian Josephus explained that the exterior of the Temple was covered in gold that reflected the fiery rays of the sun. Moreover, Josephus added that, from a distance, the Temple appeared as a mountain covered with snow.

Yeshua himself prophesied that the second Temple would be destroyed in Luke 21 :

King James Version (KJV)

5 And **as some spake of the temple**, how it was adorned with goodly stones and gifts, **he said**,
6 As for these things which ye behold, **the days will come, in the which there shall not be left one stone upon another, that shall not be thrown down**.

Around 40 years following Christ's death and resurrection, astonishingly, Yeshua's statement came to pass; not one stone stands upon another, to this day. In John 2:19-21 Christ himself substantiates our theory concerning the Temple when he tells the Jews: 'Destroy this temple, and in three days I will raise it up.' The Jews then replied to Yeshua, saying: 'It took 46 years to build this Temple, and you think you will raise it in three days?' *But Christ was referring to the resurrection of the 'temple of his body.' Which was raised in three days!*

The Third Temple will countdown the final years of mankind as we know it. Daniel discusses this 'third Temple' when he remarks, 'the prince who is to come'—the *antichrist*—will enter the Temple and stop the sacrifices in the middle of the Tribulation (Daniel 9:27).

The Apostle Paul mentions The Temple when he remarked: The 'man of lawlessness' will profane the Temple by entering it and declaring himself to be God (2 Thessalonians 2:3-4)—*again*, the 'Forbidden Fruit.' John of Patmos mentions this third Temple in his book of Revelation when he is told to 'measure' it (Revelation 11:1-2). After this *third* Temple is built, The Bible clearly states that there will be 3.5 years of 'tribulation' before The Lord comes back.

There is an apparent pattern which can be observed from studying the cycle of the rise and fall of this structure. The 'Jews' exile Jerusalem, the Temple is destroyed, Jerusalem is *re-*occupied by the 'Jews' and the cycle starts over again. And since the 'Jews' *just* 're-occupied' Israel under **British** mandate in 1948—fulfilling prophecy in Isaiah 66:8—the event which will grind the *final* ancient prophecies into place will be the construction of the third and final Temple on Temple Mount. Most of the vestments, gold candelabras, and sundries needed for the Priestly rituals have already been made and are ready to go.

There is even a giant, solid gold menorah placed right in the streets of Jerusalem in public view; the menorah is behind bullet proof glass but this is a statement which says: we *will* build the third Temple of Solomon! And if the new Temple looks anything like this giant candelabra, it will be spectacularly *terrible.* This is why Donald Trump's recent announcement that the Mount will be shared between the Philistines and the 'Jews' is so terribly disturbing.

17. Jerusalem

This postage stamp sized city was roughly one square kilometer yet, it has always commanded the attention of whoever ruled the world empire at the time, without exception, no matter how far west the center of the ruling empire was located. This goes for the United States, too, who are currently right in the center of a situation which *could* finish with the end of the world as we know it—*the sharing of Temple Mount*.

Pilgrims and Crusaders, alike, traveled thousands of miles by sea and land—at times when the heaviest price of these trips came at the cost of a large slice of one's time on this earth—just to set foot on the sacred ground of the Holy City. By this measure, it could be argued that the city itself *is* the 'Holy Grail.' But, as you now know, there *is* a single ancient treasure after which many a demonic 'knight' hath lusted.

The City of Jerusalem is the most incredible place in the world, with its history spanning into the dark voids of time. The architecture of the City was one of the most technologically advanced in the ancient world yet, academia barely notices her. Here are a couple of records which Jerusalem holds for which she never seems to get credit:

The Western Stone of the Temple of Jerusalem

Academia still disputes the fact that Solomon's Temple ever existed despite the fact that the entire foundation of the Temple still remains. The Western Wall incorporates some of the largest stones ever recorded to have been moved by man. As a matter of fact, one of the foundation stones for the Temple of Solomon, the *Western Stone*—on the *Western Wall*—is the largest stone ever to be cut by human hands, moved, and used in construction. The cut block is 570 tons; *that is, 1.25 million pounds!*

The temple of Baalbek, first dedicated to the sun 'god' baal (the demon in the Old Testament) and later dedicated to Helios—which is another evolution of the sun 'god'—in Roman times, boasts a cut stone which is even larger than the Western Stone of the Temple of Solomon. The stone is nearly double the size of the Western Stone, weighing in at just-over **1000** tons. But this stone was never 'moved, and used in construction'; it still sits in the quarry from which it was carved. The running story cites that the ancients had bit off more than they could chew; meaning, they cut a stone bigger than that which they could transport.

But I believe it's more likely that the 'giants,' for which God destroyed the world by flood, *did* build these ancient temples to satan; the fact that the 'Stone of the Pregnant Woman' of Baalbek still stands in the quarry from which it was cut must be further evidence that YHWH *did* in fact destroy the world by flood. It is a powerful image to think that real-life giants—the Nephilim of Genesis 6:4—were most-likely moving this stone at the exact moment when the skies opened up and flooded our world, preventing the stone from ever breaking the masonic record which would later be set at the Temple of Solomon.

Hezekiah's Tunnel

Though academics give Rome credit for the first aqueduct and running water, *Jerusalem* beat the Romans to this feat by 200 years! King Hezekiah of Judah was one of the Righteous Kings of Judah. Upon the Prophet Isaiah telling the King that the Babylonians would be threatening a siege on Jerusalem, Hezekiah ordered a 1750-foot tunnel carved underground to bring water from Gihon Spring to the city, hiding and therefore preserving their water source.

Below is the account of Isaiah warning King Hezekiah of an impending Babylonian siege. 2 Kings 20 :

> King James Version (KJV)
> **4** And it came to pass, afore Isaiah was gone out into the middle court, that the word of the Lord came to him, saying,
> **5** Turn again, and tell Hezekiah the captain of my people, Thus saith the Lord, the God of David thy father, I have heard thy prayer, I have seen thy tears: behold, I will heal thee: on the third day thou shalt go up unto the house of the Lord.
> **6** And I will add unto thy days fifteen years; and I will deliver thee and this city out of the hand of the king of Assyria; and I will defend this city for mine own sake, and for my servant David's sake.

Isaiah's warning prompted King Hezekiah to engineer the tunnel which would ensure the City's water source while under siege, *saving the City*. This event was documented in 2 Kings 20 :

> King James Version (KJV)
> **1** And the rest of the acts of Hezekiah, and all his might, and how **he made a pool, and a conduit, and brought water into the city,** are they not written in the book of the Chronicles of the kings of Judah?

The Siloam Inscription was found inside the tunnel which was discovered in 1838. The record documents the construction of the water conduit built by King Hezekiah, himself. The inscription found in the tunnel is the only of its kind known in the wider region to commemorate a public construction work, despite such inscriptions being commonplace in Egyptian and Mesopotamian archaeology. It is among the oldest records of its kind written in Hebrew using the Paleo-Hebrew alphabet.

The inscription contains only 6 lines; the first of which is damaged. The words are separated by dots. Keep in mind that the only word of sketchy translation is the zada on the third line :

> ... the tunnel ... and this is the story of the tunnel while ... the axes were against each other and while three cubits were left to [cut?] ... the voice of a man ... called to his counterpart, [for] there was ZADA in the rock, on the right ... and on the day of the tunnel [being finished] the stonecutters struck each man towards his counter-

part, ax against ax and flowed water from the source to the pool for 1,200 cubits. and [100?] cubits was the height over the head of the stonecutters ...

As you can see, construction of the tunnel began from both ends and the two crews of workers met in the middle with great accuracy, *just as tunnels are bored today.*

The Spring of Gihon which fed Jerusalem is a 'cold water geyser' which is *rare*; the water bubbles up from the Spring intermittently to feed the City. Since this Spring which fed Israel was the *only* water source in Jerusalem, every single citizen in Jerusalem had that water coursing through their veins. This truly makes this secret spring and underground water tunnel a 'River of Life.' The symbolism that YHWH provides us is breathtaking.

The water from Hezekiah's tunnel would fill the *Pool of Siloam* which was used to *mikveh—wash oneself before entering the Temple*. When Yeshua famously healed the blind man, the 'Great Physician's' final prescription for the man was to wash his eyes in the 'Pool of Siloam' and then he would be able to 'see.' John 9 :

> King James Version (KJV)
> **6** When he had thus spoken, he spat on the ground, and made clay of the spittle, and he anointed the eyes of the blind man with the clay,
> **7** And said unto him, **Go, wash in the pool of Siloam**. He went his way therefore, and washed, and came seeing.

Hezekiah's Tunnel is the greatest work of water engineering technology in the pre-Classical period. The Great Temple of Solomon was enormous and was one of the greatest architectural wonders of all time; it should be listed as one of the Seven Ancient Wonders but, now you know why it is not. YHWH is amazing! Is he not?

The Golden Gate

To fulfill the Biblical prophecy below, in 1541, Sultan 'Suleiman the Great' sealed off the ***eastern*** gate of Jerusalem, *also known as the* **Golden Gate**, 2000 years after the Book of Ezekiel was written. He did so after being informed that, according to Jewish tradition, the Messiah would enter Jerusalem through this gate. Suleiman built a cemetery in front of the gate as added fortification, since Jewish tradition forbade contact with the dead. Ezekiel 44 :

> King James Version (KJV)
> **1 Then he brought me back the way of the gate of the outward sanctuary which looketh toward the east**; and it was shut.
> **2** Then said the Lord unto me; **This gate shall be shut, it shall not be opened, and no man shall enter in by it; because the Lord, the God of Israel, hath entered in by it, therefore it shall be shut.**
> **3** It is for the prince; the prince, he shall sit in it to eat bread before the Lord; **he shall enter by the way of the porch of that gate, and shall go out by the way of the same.**

Suleiman's fulfillment of the prophecy above was something like a double indemnity insurance policy which would supposedly prevent the savior's return by the same gate through which he had originally rode his donkey—*customary for a King*—around a thousand and a half years prior.

The '**Golden Gate**' Bridge was placed on the *West* side of the US rather than the East as a form of rebellion, since this is in direct opposition to the position that the **Golden Gate** of Jerusalem was located. Adding to the blasphemous nature of the bridge, just like the sealed-off Golden Gate of Jerusalem, the proximity of the bridge, along with its name, is a denial of the return of Christ, since the Lord said that upon His return, He would come from the *'East'* (Mathew 24:7).

If you flip the bridge upside down, you will see that the shape of the bridge mirrors the arches of the *Golden Gate* of Jerusalem, nearly identically. 'Watergate'—*the Nixon scandal which was supposedly named for a 'hotel'*—is named for yet another gate to the City of Jerusalem.'Wall Street,' *an abomination on the other side of our country*, was named for a *street* in Jerusalem, on which the infamous 'money changers' could be found.

Another abomination worthy of mention here is a logo which is commonly referred to as the *'Golden'* Arches. If you google image the **Golden** Gate of Jerusalem, it will become quite clear to you that it is an exact match with the '**Golden**' *arches*—the logo of a 'restaurant' which has been poisoning our children with fast 'food' since 1955. This is *particularly* disturbing when you consider the fact that the idol to whom the Twelve Tribes in the Ten Commandments account were sacrificing their children was known as the **'Golden'** Calf. The guy with the red hair, wearing the hair-raising clown costume, just makes matters even worse.

18. Solomon

King Solomon is synonymous with wisdom and wealth. Any one of us can learn from this wise man, after all, he wrote several Books of The Bible. Solomon was the youngest of King David's sons; King David was one of the most respected men in The Bible.

Just as YHWH had predicted, Solomon *would* build the Temple in which to hold the Ark of the Covenant. The whole world marveled at the structure and came from every corner to behold its majesty; it was enormous. The Temple was famous for its many gold and silver utensils, candelabras and other assorted treasures. It is a good thing that Solomon became a powerful King because the whole world gleamed over this building.

From David, Solomon inherited an empire that extended from the Northeast to the Euphrates, to the southeast of the Gulf of Aqaba, and to the Southwest to the borders of Egypt and Philistia. **A great fleet of ships was amassed and trade was known to have been made as far away as Spain**.

Despite King David being such a righteous King in the eyes of The Lord, his son Solomon reverted to the old ways of idol worship. And, in spite of writing three Books of the Bible, Solomon *also* wrote a book of magic, in which he describes how to conjure up demons to assist in building an empire. The book is called the Goetia. Muslims also believe that Solomon had dominion over demons with which he moved those 570 ton stones; and they *still* perceive Solomon as a 'prophet'—a 'good' guy.

Despite Solomon starting out his reign as one of the Greatest Kings of The Bible, his descent into perdition was particularly gross. After falling from YHWH's grace, Solomon kept up to 700 wives and 300 concubines in his harem. In fact, Solomon also built a great Temple to Molech with which to attract young ladies from the corners of his empire, so they could meet him as they passed their offspring through the glowing arms of the metal statue.

Solomon broke his promise to YHWH and so it was at the cost of striped backs for his people. (I believe that the stripes on the American flag actually symbolize the slavery of our people. Stars have always represented 'gods' or 'kings' and stripes in The Bible represent slavery and oppression.) Even though Solomon began his reign as a righteous ruler, in the eyes of YHWH, he too couldn't resist the bitter fruit of becoming god of his subjective universe.

King Solomon was famous for his copper mines and forgeries long before our Civil Wars, 'revolutions,' and World Wars, which generate money and industry for *our* corrupt metal foundries. Solomon was a great king of commerce for an expanding empire, of which Jerusalem was the Capital City. Sadly, Solomon was running the same exact timeworn game as King Nimrod.

The cost of maintaining Solomon's court had outpaced his economic engine—exactly like the US has done today—and before long, the great empire began to display financial fissures in its many foundations. Many of Solomon's great buildings were at the cost of '*striped*-backs' for his people, who became more and more enslaved as his empire withered; *just like ours is doing.*

The Bible tells of Solomon's coronation which, remarkably, is identical to that of the Royal Family of Windsor. Perhaps it should be said that it *is* the same exact coronation as Solomon's since they are of the same bloodline; below is but a short list of rituals with which to demonstrate this point :

—During the coronation of a British monarch, the people shout 'god save the king! Long live the king!' Corresponding verse in I Samuel 10 :

> King James Version (KJV)
> **24** And Samuel said to all the people, See ye him whom the Lord hath chosen, that there is none like him among all the people? **And all the people shouted, and said, God save the king.**

—The forehead of the prospective *royal* is anointed with oil in the shape of an 'X.' After which, the new King or Queen of Britain is considered to be one of 'the gods.' I Kings 1 :

King James Version (KJV)

39 And Zadok **the priest took an horn of oil out of the tabernacle, and anointed Solomon**. And they blew the trumpet; **and all the people said, God save king Solomon**.

Right around the time of this 'anointing' with oil, there is a secret ritual which is *not* aired on television. Perhaps this is a creepy ritual similar to that of The Order of Skull and Bones in which they invite evil spirits to work through them, like the first King of Judah, King Saul.

—As aforementioned, to this day, British monarchs are crowned upon the 'Stone of Scone,' also known as 'Jacob's Pillow.' Remember, *Jacob's Pillow* was the stone on which Jacob's head rested while having his fateful *Jacob's Ladder* dream; in this dream, 'angels' came-and-went in-and-out of our world, at their leisure. Legend has it that as long as the monarch is crowned upon this stone, they will remain in power. This legend fits the following Biblical prophecy perfectly: Genesis 49 :

King James Version (KJV)

10 The sceptre shall not depart from Judah, nor a lawgiver from between his feet, until Shiloh come; and unto him shall the gathering of the people be.

Modern scientists claim to have disproven that *Jacob's Pillow* and the *Stone of Scone*—on which the royals are crowned—are one-in-the-same but, I see no reason to subscribe to such transparent and false claims, when such damnatory historical evidence all seems to point to their own 'legends' as *matters of fact*.

—The crown which is placed on the new ruler's head is mounted with Twelve **jew**els to represent the Twelve Tribes of Israel who they preside over, *mimicking the Breastplate of Judgment*—the *Holy Grail*. Exodus 28 :

> King James Version (KJV)
> **21 And the stones shall be with the names of the children of Israel, twelve, according to their names**, like the engravings of a signet; every one with his name shall they be according to the twelve tribes.

The throne of David, upon which the British royals are crowned, is placed upon a pyramid of six steps. 1 Kings 10 :

> King James Version (KJV)
> **19** The throne had six steps, and the top of the throne was round behind: and there were stays on either side on the place of the seat, and two lions stood beside the stays.

So, to clarify: our basic unit of currency, the one dollar bill, displays a pyramid which is missing its top and the British kings are *all* crowned upon the *top* of a six-stepped pyramid.

Just think, we will get to see this ancient, Biblical, coronation in our lifetime, when the queen passes and the next in this unbroken chain of kings is crowned. The coronation of the next king of Judah—*British Monarch*—will stand as only the second time that this event has ever been filmed and televised in the history of mankind.

19. System of the Beast

Revelation tells of the ultimate one world antichrist system. Roughly two thousand years ago, John of Patmos described a system in which one evil man would rise up and declare *himself* to be 'god.' This 'antichrist'—'the beast'—will go on to number us with a 'mark' on our 'hand' or on our 'head.' It is said in Revelation that no man would be granted the ability to buy or sell without having this 'mark of the beast.' Revelation 13 :

> King James Version (KJV)
> **15** And **he had power to give life unto the image of the beast, that the image of the beast should both speak, and cause that as many as would not worship the image of the beast should be killed.**
> **16** And **he causeth all, both small and great, rich and poor, free and bond, to receive a mark in their right hand, or in their foreheads:**
> **17 And that no man might buy or sell, save he that had the mark**, or the name of the beast, or the number of his name.
> **18 Here is wisdom. Let him that hath understanding count the number of the beast: for it is the number of a man; and his number is Six hundred threescore and six.**

Verse 18, *above*, states '**here is wisdom**,' let him that hath understanding count the number of the beast: **for it is the number of a man**; **and his number is Six hundred threescore and six**. It is no wonder that the freemasons who love symology would also love *The Bible*. The bit of symology, in verse 18 in particular, ironically fingers their precious **King Solomon** as being '**the beast**,' or at least the 'system of the beast.'

That verse 18 above *also* states, '**Let him that hath understanding count the number of the beast**,' states that we have already been told the information we need to know in order to solve the mystery of the number 666; you only ask someone if they 'understand' you if you've already provided them with a cursory explanation of the idea in question—it is a riddle for which we *have* been given the information to solve and we will, *below*.

When reading the passage below, *remember*, **King Solomon** *is* the 'wisest man in The Bible.' Look at 1 Kings 4 :

> King James Version (KJV)
> **30** And **Solomon's wisdom** excelled the **wisdom** of all the children of the east country, and all the wisdom of Egypt.

King Solomon, in his Biblical worldwide search for wisdom, must certainly have come across Nimrod's esoteric knowledge of becoming god of one's society, which Solomon just couldn't resist. You can even hear Solomon's faith teetering as he writes in Ecclesiastes 1 :

King James Version (KJV)
18 For in much wisdom is much grief: and he that increaseth knowledge increaseth sorrow.

Solomon drivels endlessly about the woes caused by wisdom and, looking back, it makes perfect sense. This man was on the edge of joining the side of antichrist and rejecting the beloved YHWH who cherished Solomon and his father, King David.

Revelation 13:18—which points to 666 being the 'number of the beast'— corresponds with two other scriptures in two separate books of The Bible which point to Solomon a second and even a third time in a total of *three separate Books* of the Bible! Kings and Chronicles :

1 Kings 10:14 King James Version (KJV)
14 Now the weight of gold that came to **Solomon** in one year was **six hundred threescore and six talents of gold,**

2 Chronicles 9 King James Version (KJV)
13 Now the weight of gold that came to **Solomon** in one year was **six hundred and threescore and six talents of gold**; ...

Note: Verse 13 above is another 'neon sign' since the very next verse states that there was way more additional gold going to Solomon: '*Beside that which chapmen and merchants brought. And all the kings of Arabia and governors of the country brought gold and silver to Solomon.*'

It is fascinating that the writers of these three books of The Bible, centuries apart, encoded this amazing Revelation which was meant for us to use in order to identify the system of antichrist. And, if you think about it, it makes perfect sense. There was surely some form of this same system in their times and perhaps, these men even, at some point, belonged to ancient evolutions of these same clandestine clubs. They could have changed their ways and, beyond the message with which *YHWH* had entrusted them, maybe they at one time held the mystery knowledge, themselves, but changed their ways.

Paul was one such antichrist who terrorized and killed Christians on the Road to Damascus, not long after the Romans cornered Christ and nailed him to a tree. Paul would certainly have been a member of the *sons of darkness* and therefore familiar with their creed. Paul repented of his crimes against Christ and went on to write most of the New Testament; Paul then travelled the same roads where before he had stoned Christians to death, spreading the Buds of God's Word to much of the ancient world *which then blossomed into ours*. This shows that any one of us can enter into YHWH's Order if we so choose, regardless of our iniquities.

One Eye Imagery
The 'all-seeing eye' is powerful imagery that we now see everywhere and it isn't anything new. Most believe that the concept began with the 'all-seeing eye of Horus' or the 'Eye of Ra' in Egypt, *but*, as you will now learn, it goes back even further.

From Egypt, the *eye of Horus* was inherited by the new evolution of the Roman Emperors—*the pope*—and its symbology can be found carved in stone on the facades of Catholic churches all over the world. The Bible confirms this 'one eye imagery,' in which the Biblical antichrist is also described as having an eye which has been 'darkened,' in Zechariah 11 :

> King James Version (KJV)
>
> [16] For, lo, I will raise up a shepherd in the land, which shall not visit those that be cut off, neither shall seek the young one, nor heal that that is broken, nor feed that that standeth still: but he shall eat the flesh of the fat, and tear their claws in pieces.
>
> [17] Woe to the idol shepherd that leaveth the flock! **the sword shall be upon his arm, and upon his right eye**: his arm shall be clean dried up, and **his right eye shall be utterly darkened**.

The Norse Vikings took this 'evil eye' with them when they floated through the British Isles spreading bloodshed and conquering those lands, with their evolution of this imagery: the Norse 'god' *Odin, who was blind in one eye.*

And, finally, East India Company revived this old magic eye, in the form of what we have come to know as a 'pirate.' Our kids now run wild on halloween wearing this dumb eye patch while collecting pounds and pounds of processed sugar. Pirates dressed in red, Russell—the surname of the family who founded the secret society 'The Order of Skull and Bones' means 'red'—and the pirate's black flag is emblazoned with Yale's precious 'Skull and Bones.' Isis, S&B's new invented enemy, now shares their black and white flag configuration. But, back to the original statement made about this 'eye': Where did it originate?

Yup! You guessed it, according to ancient Jewish records, when Nimrod was informed that Abraham had come forth from Nimrod's hot furnace uninjured, he ceased his persecution of the followers of YHWH; however, on the following night a dream revealed a man exiting the hot furnace after which he approached Nimrod with a drawn sword.

Nimrod took off, but the man tossed an egg at him; the egg was transformed into a large river in which all of Nimrod's troops were drowned; only Nimrod and three of his men escaped the powerful torrent. Then the river returned to its original shape—*that of a tiny egg*—and from the latter came forth **a small bird which flew at Nimrod and pecked his eye out**.

The Muslims have a similar tradition in which the *Ad-Dajjal*—or, *antichrist*—is *blind* in his right eye, which looks like a bulging grape. Ali—son-in-law of *Muhammad*—was reported to have said: 'His right eye will be punctured, and his left eye would be raised to his forehead and will be sparkling like a star.'

When you purchase that bag of chips on your next feeding break at 'work,' I would like for you to look down at the symbolism on your one dollar bill before you stick it in the lighted slot. While doing so, meditate on the following few items:

—King Nimrod's invention, the *'pyramid,'* is situated to the left side on the reverse of this worthless document.

—Just above the pyramid which is missing its top, you have King Nimrod's *one* good eye staring at you.

—On the right side of the document, you have an eagle; I would like for you to recall the story of *Zeus* and *Prometheus* while you're staring at the eagle on that dollar in your hand. In *that* story, the beast, *'Prometheus'*—Nimrod—*repeatedly* regenerates a new liver which the eagle would fly down and eat, *in perpetuity*.

This means that the 'pyramid' on the left side of your dollar bill features the Tower of Babel, above which the eye of Nimrod stares back at you. To the right side of your dollar is an eagle which represents the perpetual return of this antichrist; let us not forget that the pyramid on the dollar bill is missing its top and the British kings are *all* crowned upon the *top* of a pyramid. Under the Tower of Babel reads: *'Out of many, one'* : *e pluribus unum in Roman speak (Latin)*. A variant of this phrase was used in *Moretum*, a poem attributed to Virgil, a man whose hand has now reached our own times from thousands of years in the past; more on this later when we discuss the new Tower of Babel and Apollonian Complex: **One World Trade Center**.

One more note on this topic: The *eagle* was the empirical symbol for every major empire described in Daniel, along with that of King Solomon, as well as being that of Nazi Germany and now America.

20. Daniel's Empirical Prophecy

Jermeiah Holmes Wiffen wrote the book, *Memoirs of the House of Russell: From the Time of the Norman **Conquest***, which is the work on which the thesis of my first book written under the pseudonym 'Judah' was based. The book was chartered by John 6th Duke of Bedford, so it was written by *no* conspiracy 'theorist.' *Duke,* is the highest member of the royal bloodline outside of the actual King or Queen.

Duke John hired his librarian, *poet, Jeremiah Holmes Wiffen* to research and write the tell-all document, which draws great parallels between my *nonfiction* books and the invented *Da Vinci Code*. It is quite apparent that the Da Vinci Code was simply the fictitious version of the hidden truth which you are finally reading now; *it was just another intentional detour for truth seekers*. Wiffen's book was never meant to be studied by the common man; it was created to document the many conquests of the forerunners to the British throne for 'posterity,' but the book was only intended for readers who were close relatives to the throne.

The work chronicles the Russell families' sinister conquests, back to the very start of recorded human history; this is the same *Russell family* which produced *William Huntington Russell* who founded *Yale's, Order of Skull and Bones—the fraternity which worships skulls*. The book places the royal family in the wrong places, at the wrong times, for the destruction of countless peoples, of many races, of which there doesn't seem to be any level of discrimination.

This means that the royal family *themselves* documented *their own* ruthless conquests, throughout history; from their ancestry of *viking kings* to their secret role in the *Crusades* as the *Knights Templar* to *William the Conquerer's* 'conquest' of *Britain; it is truly breathtaking.*

There were only 250 original copies of this 'little book' produced to ensure that the publication didn't fall into the wrong hands but it still did; in our times, some unsuspecting librarian must've mindlessly uploaded the historic document without realizing its damning historical significance.

Once you read the old book for yourself, you quickly realize that Wiffen was fascinated by the exploits documented in the ancient archives of the royals, but that he also understood the prophetic implications of what he was reading and writing; Wiffen wrote *many* hidden clues beneath the surface of the passages chosen. But it was one single line in Wiffen's book that opened the door to the entire text you are reading now; it was as if Wiffen was sending me a desperate clue, from hundreds of years in the past, when he wrote :

'**The iron and the clay in the feet of the prophetic image of empire**, is an apt and instructive emblem of the brute force, or of the crumbling policies, which have been constantly employed by the governors of human kind, **in every modern division of the old theatre of Roman domination.**'

When reading the Russell '*Memoirs* book,' I could tell that this was a quote but, I am embarrassed to say that I *didn't* know *what* was being quoted. A quick google search turned up the *Book of Daniel* and his prophetic interpretation of *King Nebuchadnezzar's Dream*. Daniel's interpretation of the king's infamous dream remarkably depicts the rise and fall of every single world empire beginning with *Babylon* which is where this account is set. Below, *I* paraphrased the Daniel account into our modern vernacular for your reading enjoyment :

Daniel was a noble of Jewish blood who *lived* in Jerusalem when Nebuchadnezzar sieged the Holy City and destroyed the Temple of Solomon. And, just as with 'Operation Paperclip' following WWII, anyone considered to be a keeper of knowledge—*in 'science' or otherwise*—after the City and Temple were destroyed, were marched back to Babylon for whatever use they may be to the King. Daniel was a great *interpreter of dreams*—a *Prophet*—so his services would've been coveted in times when man still had respect for spirituality.

Following *Nebuchadnezzar's* siege on Jerusalem, the powerful and evil king had his famous dream. The king commanded all of the magicians, astrologers, and the sorcerers, to interpret his prophetic dream. So they came and stood before the king.

Nebuchadnezzar turned to the soothsayers and shouted, 'show me the interpretation of my dream and you will be showered with gifts and honor but if you cannot I shall cut you to pieces!' The group asked the king to describe what he saw while he slept but the king couldn't recall the scene. The Babylonian soothsayers answered the king, saying, 'There isn't a man on earth who could tell you what your dream means without even knowing what you saw.'

This made the king furious, so he commanded that all of the magicians in Babylon be slain. Though Daniel was one of the good guys, he was bunched up with the soothsayers to be killed, when Daniel spoke up to the captain of the king's royal guard and said: '*I can interpret the king's dream.*'

Then the secret of the evil king's dream was revealed unto Daniel in a night vision and Daniel prayed with thanksgiving to YHWH, the God of Heaven: Daniel answered saying, 'Blessed be the name of YHWH for ever and ever: for wisdom and might are His. He changes the times and the seasons, He removes kings and makes kings, He imparts wisdom unto those who seek it, and knowledge to those who seek knowledge. YHWH reveals the deeply secret things, He knows what is in the darkness, and the light dwells within Him. Thank you, YHWH, for revealing to me the king's dream.'

Therefore Daniel went in to see Nebuchadnezzar's captain and said: 'Please do not destroy the wise men of Babylon *(Daniel, his pals from Jerusalem, and all of the other magicians and soothsayers in Babylon).* Take me to the king, and *I* will interpret his dream.'

Then Arioch hastily brought Daniel before the king, and said, 'I have found a man of the captives of Judah, that will interpret the meaning of your dream even though you don't even remember it.' The king answered Daniel, whose name was changed to *Belteshazzar* by the Babylonians: 'Art thou able to interpret my dream?' Daniel answered in the presence of the king, saying: 'All of the wise men, astrologers, magicians and soothsayers, cannot interpret your dream but there is a God in heaven that reveals secrets, and He will make known to you, O king, what will unfold in the latter days.

'In your dream the following occurred: O king, you beheld a great statue which was bright and excellent but it was that of a terrible king. This great image, whose brightness was excellent, stood before thee; and the form thereof was terrible. The head of the image was made of gold, his breast and his arms were made of silver, his belly and thighs were made of brass, his legs were made of iron, and his feet were made partly of iron and part of clay.

'You watched the statue, O king, until a stone with arms which appeared to be cut without hands, struck the image upon his feet which were made of iron and clay, and broke the whole thing to pieces. The iron, clay, brass, silver, and the gold, were pulverized to dust and became like the chaff of the summer threshingfloors;

the wind carried them away and no place was found for them; the stone that smote the image became a great mountain and filled the whole earth.

'That was your dream and here is the interpretation thereof: O king, your kingdom is the head of gold. But your kingdom will be overthrown by one inferior to yours. And a third kingdom of brass shall rule over all of the earth. And the fourth kingdom will become as strong as iron: forasmuch as iron breaks to pieces and conquers all things.

'The feet and toes were made partly of potters' clay and part iron; so this kingdom will be divided but will have the strength of iron mixed with miry clay. And just as the toes were iron mixed with clay, so too shall this fourth kingdom be partly strong but partly weak. But, the iron and clay will not stick together, **they shall mingle themselves with the seed of men**: but they shall not cleave one to another, just as iron will not mix with clay.

'**And in the days of these kings,** *God of heaven will spread the Word of God to His people* in order to establish His kingdom which shall never be destroyed: and the kingdom will not be left to other men; it shall break in pieces and consume all these kingdoms and stand for ever.'

King Nebuchadnezzar fell on his face and began to worship Daniel and began commanding his people to serve Daniel with gifts. The evil king Nebuchadnezzar then agreed that Daniel's God was the God of gods, and King of kings, and a revealer of secrets, since He showed Daniel the meaning of Nebuchadnezzar's dream. The king made Daniel a great man, and gave him many great gifts, and even made him ruler over the whole province of Babylon, and chief of the governors over all the wise men of Babylon.

But we know that Nebuchadnezzar's admiration for YHWH would soon fade since, we see that in the very next Chapter of Daniel—*in Chapter 3*—Nebuchadnezzar **builds** this enormous statue whom is most-likely king Nimrod, and orders that every person in Babylon should bow before the statue when they hear a series of musical instruments being sounded. Daniel and a few of his righteous pals, *Shadrach*, *Meshach*, and *Abednego*, would have *none* of this; the four refused to worship the image. Below is more of my paraphrasing, this time in Daniel Chapter 3 :

When brought before Nebuchadnezzar, Shadrach, Meshach, and Abednego, said to the king, 'O Nebuchadnezzar, our God whom we serve will deliver us from your fiery furnace, and he will deliver us out of your hands, as well, O king. *O king*, we will *not* serve your gods, nor worship the golden image which thou hast set up. Then Nebuchadnezzar became exceedingly angry, and the form of his temper was changed toward Shadrach, Meshach, and Abednego, and he commanded that they should heat the furnace seven times hotter than it had been heated. And he commanded the most mighty men that were in his army to bind Shadrach, Meshach, and Abednego, and to cast them into the burning fiery furnace.

The three righteous men were bound in the clothes they were wearing, their coats, their hosen, and even still wearing their hats when they were cast into the fiery furnace. Because the king's commandment was urgent, and the furnace exceedingly hot, the flames of the fire *killed* the men who escorted Shadrach, Meshach, and Abednego into the flames. And these three men fell down, *bound*, into the midst of the burning fiery furnace.

Then king Nebuchadnezzar became astonished, and rose up in haste, as he shouted to his counsellors: 'Did not we cast the three bound men into the hot fire?' They answered unto the king, '*True*, O king.' The king answered saying, 'I see four men loose, walking in the midst of the fire, and they have not been harmed; **and the form of the fourth is like the Son of God**.'

Then Nebuchadnezzar came near the mouth of the fiery furnace, and spoke, and *shouted*, '*Shadrach, Meshach*, and *Abednego*, ye servants of the most high God, come forth, and come here!' Then Shadrach, Meshach, and Abednego, came forth of the midst of the fire.

And the princes, governors, captains, king's and counsellors were gathered together, and saw that these mens' bodies were preserved; not a hair of their head was singed, neither were their coats changed; the three didn't even smell like smoke. Then Nebuchadnezzar spoke, saying, 'Blessed be the God of Shadrach, Meshach, and Abednego, who hath sent his angel to deliver his servants who trusted in him so that they might not serve nor worship any god, except their own God.

'Therefore I make a decree, That every people, nation, and language, which speak any wrong word against the God of Shadrach, Meshach, and Abednego, shall be cut in pieces, and their houses shall be made a dunghill: because there is no other god that can deliver after this sort.'

The account above in Daniel gives us a sneak peak at the antichristian establishment of the end times; it is a perfect analogue for the scriptures in the Book of Revelation which also describes these same ominous times. Revelation 13 :

King James Version (KJV)
15 And he had power to give life unto the image of the beast, that the image of the beast should both speak, and cause that as many as would not worship the image of the beast should be killed.

Remarkably, It appears as if John could foresee that our generation would have the technology to bring this image to 'life,' *and what a terrible thought*. But the next 'image' will simply be a high-tech spin on the same forces of evil which have risen to the top of every world empire from day one.

As you will see in the forthcoming chapters, every single empire from the beginning of time until the end, were all predicted by YHWH through

Daniel, by way of Nebuchadnezzar's dream. The excerpts above were paraphrased in modern speak for ease of reading. You should read them yourself to confirm your interpretation but, I am sure you will have trouble keeping your hands off of The Bible, from now forward.

21. I Head of Gold—Babylon

History was always an enigma to me before becoming familiar with the miraculous symbolism hidden in plain sight within *The Word of God*. YHWH's perfect plan includes a History Book which miraculously illustrates the History of the World using a rudimentary statue of the human form—the *statue* in *Nebuchadnezzar's dream* which was interpreted by YHWH's righteous servant, *Daniel*.

This symbolism provided a simple memorization tool with which to remember most of the major events of world history. Think of that: The greatest tool imaginable for mentally logging and recalling the world's undisputed history of world dominion comes from a prophecy which was written long before these major world events *had even occurred!*

As stated in the last chapter, each segment of the statue represented the birth of a new world empire. Putting aside the antediluvian world which we know little of, *Babylon* was the first world empire and it was represented by the 'head of gold,' followed by the 'arms and chest of silver' which represent the conquest of Babylon by the *Medo-Persians*. The third empire was the rise of the *Greek* empire, and finally, *Rome* rises to its terrible power, being represented by the terrible statue's '*legs of iron*'—the 'fourth empire.'

A fifth empire which will be struck by a big '*stone*' is represented by the feet made of 'iron mixed with clay.' We will get into great detail describing this empire in later chapters.

Empire I Babylon

As stated in the past chapter, Nebuchadnezzar's *Babylon*, was an evolution of the first world empire. We have discussed Babylon in great detail so, I will use the next blank page to give you a mental image of what Babylonian life looked like around the same times as Daniel; well, at least within a couple hundred years of Daniel's times.

You know, to me Babylon has simply been a word—a lost civilization of which we all know very little about. But, unbelievably, and probably unbeknownst to you, we know more about mankind's earliest empire than we do nearly any other ancient ruins on this earth. These people recorded *everything* on clay tablets! *Everything!* The earliest historians visited this place too and their dusty writings are simply ignored.

As a gift to you, I am going to include a writing from the 'father of history,' '*Herodotus!*' Herodotus visited ancient Babylon and even beheld her ancient wonder: *The Hanging Gardens of Babylon*. But it's not the botanical gardens of Babylon to which I wish to charm your attention.

Below is an account from Herodotus which shows just one of the many ugly consequences of this same evil, which can creep up on any society.

And now, ancient Babylon comes alive for you with the account of Herodotus upon his visit to the infamous, Biblical City :

> The foulest Babylonian custom is that which compels every woman of the land to sit in the temple of Aphrodite and have intercourse with some stranger at least once in her life. Many women who are rich and proud and disdain to mingle with the rest, drive to the temple in covered carriages drawn by teams, and stand there with a great retinue of attendants. But most sit down in the sacred plot of Aphrodite, with crowns of cord on their heads; there is a great multitude of women coming and going; passages marked by line run every way through the crowd, by which the men pass and make their choice.
>
> Once a woman has taken her place there, she does not go away to her home before some stranger has cast money into her lap, and had intercourse with her outside the temple; but while he casts the money, he must say, 'I invite you in the name of *Mylitta*.' It does not matter what sum the money is; the woman will never refuse, for that would be a sin, the money being by this act made sacred. So she follows the first man who casts it and rejects no one.
>
> After their intercourse, having discharged her sacred duty to the goddess, she goes away to her home; and thereafter there is no bribe however great that will get her. So then the women that are fair and tall are soon free to depart, but the uncomely have long to wait because they cannot fulfil the law; for some of them remain for

three years, or four. There is a custom like this in some parts of Cyprus.

The Babylon described by Herodotus, above, is a far tamer place than that of Daniel's times but this gives us a peak into the depravity that festers in a society, and which eventually does (did) evolve into a system of antichrist.

Just as with Joseph—*one of the Twelve sons of Jacob—Daniel's* correct interpretation of a king's dream elevated himself to a high-ranking status in a kings court, but this time it was on the stage of a world empire. This was the beginning of the Hebrews' infiltration of the thrones of the entire world; and they all owed their glory to YHWH but, in the end, they just couldn't resist the temptation of the Forbidden Fruit—*playing 'god.'*

To end Nebuchadnezzar's wickedness, Daniel again interpreted one of the king's dreams which foretold of his going mad and living in the wilderness, eating grass like an 'ox,' and finally, growing 'feathers' and 'talons' like an 'eagle.'

If you google image 'William Blake Nebuchadnezzar,' you will see one of Poet, William Blake's watercolors in which a long-haired Nebuchadnezzar is crawling around the wilderness, sprouting feathers and claws; it is Blake's concept of the above event.

William Blake was a pal of Wiffen's—*the author of the royal 'tell-all' book*—and he was even mentioned in Wiffen's book. The two lived in an industrialized London during the early 1800s, which was particularly gross. Blake even wrote a poem which became London's de facto anthem, and it is still played before sporting events there, to this day. If you listen to the lyrics of *And Did Those Feet in Ancient Time*, it will become quite clear to you that Blake's disgust with the goings-on of the day disturbed him terribly.

Blake even wrote a series of books that are referred to as the 'Prophetic Books' which, I am sure hold similar disenfranchised tidings. Blake's artwork mirrored his disgust of the times and his depiction of Nebuchadnezzar growing the feathers and claws of an eagle was no exception.

If you google image the word '*Anunnaki*,' you will see from these images of 'the gods,' raised on stone reliefs—*found in the archaeological sites of ancient Babylon—that most of them had 'feathers' and 'eagle claws!'* They looked like, well, *fallen angels*. Perhaps this was another manifestation of the *Nephilim* genes spoken-of in Genesis: Nebuchadnezzar may have literally began to become as 'the gods' ; Nebuchadnezzar's name even means, *'O god, Nabu.'*

After 'seven years' of madness and living in the wilderness among the animals, Nebuchadnezzar finally turned his heart toward YHWH. Look at Daniel 4 :

> King James Version (KJV)
> **34 And at the end of the days I Nebuchadnezzar lifted up mine eyes unto heaven, and mine understanding returned unto me, and I blessed the most High, and I praised and honoured him**

that liveth for ever, whose dominion is an everlasting dominion, and his kingdom is from generation to generation:
35 And all the inhabitants of the earth are reputed as nothing: and he doeth according to his will in the army of heaven, and among the inhabitants of the earth: and none can stay his hand, or say unto him, What doest thou?

The satire in all of this is: Nearly every single preacher on this planet thinks the absolute world of *Solomon* whom The Bible makes *no* mention of his repentance for his terrible atrocities, and, *Nebuchadnezzar—the horrible tyrant who threw YHWH's Prophets inside a hot furnace*—will probably be the one sitting next to you, dabbing the corners of his mouth at the *Great Feast!*

22. II Medo-Persia—the Writing on the Wall

Daniel stated in his interpretation of Nebuchadnezzar's dream that the empire following his would be inferior to Babylon; *and Daniel was right. Belshazzar, Nebuchadnezzar's son*, would return to idolatry, general wickedness, and human sacrifice, and it was *he* who would bring about the end of the great Babylonian reign of the ancient world. The following account from Daniel is, again, paraphrased, this time from Chapter 5 :

> King Belshazzar, the final king of the Babylonian empire, threw a great feast and invited a thousand of his highest ranked men along with a few others, who all proceeded to get drunk with wine. After tasting the wine, king Belshazzar commanded that they fetch the gold and silver vessels which his father Nebuchadnezzar had looted from Jerusalem before his forces utterly destroyed the Temple of Solomon; the king ordered the vessels so he and his cronies might continue drinking from them.

> They brought in the golden vessels and the king, his princes, his wives, and his concubines, all began to drink from the cups from the Temple. They drank their wine and praised the 'gods of gold and silver, brass, iron, wood and of stone.'

In the same hour, the fingers of a mysterious hand began writing upon the plaister of the wall in the king's palace. Then the king's face went blank with the look of astonishment and his knees began to knock together. The king cried aloud to bring in the astrologers and the soothsayers, just as his father had done after having his famous dream.

The king spoke, saying to the wise men of Babylon, 'whoever can read and interpret this writing shall be placed third in charge of the entire kingdom.' All of the wise men crowded the writing upon the wall but no one even understood the words, *much less their interpretation*. King Belshazzar became greatly troubled, and it seemed to worry his governors, as well.

After overhearing the ruckus of the party, the queen entered into the banquet room and spoke, saying, 'O king, live for ever and don't worry about that; don't let it bother you in the least. There is a man in thy kingdom who would impart wisdom and understanding of these matters to your father. His interpretations were so accurate that your father gave him dominion over all of the soothsayers for whom you sent. His name is *Daniel* and he will provide the interpretation of this mysterious writing on the wall.

Then Daniel was brought before the king. And the king spoke to Daniel: 'Are you *the* Daniel of the Tribe of Judah who was captured from Jerusalem by my father? I am told that you give interpretations without error: *now,* if you can read the writing on the wall and tell me what it means, I will clothe you in red, wrap a nice gold chain around your neck, and you will be the third ruler in the kingdom.' Daniel answered, saying before the king :

'You can keep your gifts, or just give them to someone else but, I will read the mysterious writing and tell you what it all means.

'O king, the most high God gave your father, *Nebuchadnezzar,* a great kingdom, and majesty, and glory and honor. And he used that majesty, *which the Almighty God had gifted to your father*, to cause all people, from all nations and languages, to tremble with fear before him; he was a brutal king and tortured and killed people until God sent him to the wilderness where he became mad until his heart was softened by the Almighty.

'And *you, Belshazzar*, have not humbled *your* heart, and *you knew all of this*; you have placed yourself in the way of the will of God in Heaven; and you have used the vessels from *His* house, and you have proceeded to become drunk by drinking wine from them while praising your idols of silver and gold, brass, iron, wood and stone. These idols cannot see, hear, or understand you. But the God whose very breath is in your hands, *you have not glorified.*'

Then, the rest of the hand belonging to the fingers which had written on the wall appeared, and the following words became legible:

'**Mene, Mene, Tekel, Upharsin.**'

After the words became legible, Daniel solved the mystery saying: 'And here is the interpretation of those words:

—'**Mene**; God has numbered your kingdom and *it is finished*.

—'**Tekel**; Thou art weighed in the balances, *and art found wanting*.

—'**Peres**; Thy kingdom will be divided and given to the Medes and Persians.'

Then Belshazzar commanded that his servants clothe Daniel with scarlet and to give him that gold chain he had promised the Prophet. The king then made a proclamation concerning Daniel, making him third in charge of the entire empire.

But Belshazzar and Daniel's co-kingship would be very short-lived, for that very night Belshazzar, the king of Babylon was slain, and *Darius* the *Median* took the kingdom at the age of 62 years old.

The history of the above account is all documented. The first of Daniel's empirical predictions had come to pass. But, incredibly, The Bible had already predicted this changing of the guard in Isaiah 44 :

> King James Version (KJV)
> **28** That saith of *Cyrus*, **He is my shepherd, and shall perform all my pleasure**: even saying to Jerusalem, **Thou shalt be built; and to the temple, Thy foundation shall be laid**.

With impeccable accuracy, Isaiah had not only predicted that the Persians would rebuild the Temple which Nebuchadnezzar had knocked down but, *Isaiah* had even *named the Persian King* who'd lead the siege on Babylon when this world empire fell into the clutches of the *Medo-Persians*. When God speaks of *Cyrus* 'performing His pleasure,' it is because he would re-institute the occupation of Jerusalem which Nebuchadnezzar had *undone*.

Isaiah wrote the above passage somewhere around 175 years prior to the *Medo-Persian* siege of Babylon. The Book of Ezra describes in great detail that the older men 'wept' when they watched the 'laying of the foundations.' Look at Ezra 3 :

> King James Version (KJV)
> **12** But many of the priests and Levites and chief of the fathers, who were ancient men, that had seen the first house, **when the foundation of this house was laid before their eyes, wept with a loud voice;** and many shouted aloud for joy: ...

If you will notice, the 'weeping' of the older men seems to be for a completely different reason than those who 'shouted aloud for joy' ; the sentence is even separated by a semicolon, implying two separate ideas ; perhaps these old men were well aware that the Temple would again be used for *evil*. The running academic interpretation of this verse is that these men were shouting for *joy*. But it really *doesn't* matter; it is just fun to contemplate. The real value in this account is in the accuracy with which prophetic events unfolded.

The Medes are *first* mentioned in Scripture when Isaiah 13:17 prophetically declared, *175 years before being fulfilled*, 'Behold, I will stir up the Medes against them, which shall not regard silver; and as for gold, they shall not delight in it.' Subsequently, in Isaiah 13:19, he again predicts Babylon's downfall when he says, 'And Babylon, the glory of kingdoms, the beauty of the Chaldees' excellency, shall be as when God overthrew Sodom and Gomorrah.'

Jeremiah 51:11, reveals that the Medes will be used by God to destroy Babylon, when he says: 'Make bright the arrows; gather the shields: the Lord hath raised up the spirit of the kings of the Medes: for his device is against Babylon, to destroy it; because it is the vengeance of the Lord, the vengeance of his Temple.'

It seems that even though He didn't determine that the building of the Temple was a good idea in the beginning, it was still *YHWH's House*, and He was determined to take back what was his!

23. III - IV — Greece / Rome

Alexander III was also known as *Alexander the Great*. He was a king of Macedon who was born in 356 BC, succeeding his father at the young age of 20. The young king was a great warrior and spent the first of his ruling years doing-so from the theater of war while ripping through Asia and northeast Africa. Alexander had already brought most of the known world under his power by the age of thirty. His breadth of conquest was one of the greatest military campaigns of all time and he is still revered, today, by military strategists throughout the world.

In his 'greatness,' Alexander would be the guy who would fulfill Daniel's prophecies, with great accuracy. Daniel 8 gives specific details of the clash that would bring the Medo-Persian empire to its knees.

The ancient historians Herodotus and Xenophon record that the Persian king Cyrus focused his conquest **westward** to the Aegean Sea, **north** into Cappadocia and Armenia, and **southward** into Egypt. These events are to the letter what Daniel had predicted would happen. Look at Daniel 8 :

> King James Version (KJV)
> **4 I saw the ram pushing westward**, and **northward**, and **southward**; so that no beasts might stand before him, neither was there

any that could deliver out of his hand; but he did according to his will, and **became *great*.**

Look at the last word of the scripture above which matches Alexander's epithet, *exactly; Alexander the **Great***. Then in the very next passage we see an incredibly accurate prediction of the way things unfolded for Alexander. Again, Daniel 8 :

King James Version (KJV)
5 And as I was considering, behold, **an he goat came from the west** on the face of the whole earth, **and touched not the ground**: and **the goat had a notable horn between his eyes**.
6 And he came to the ram that had two horns [Media and Persia], which I had seen standing before the river, and ran unto him in the fury of his power.
7 And I saw him come close unto the ram, and he was moved with choler against him, **and smote the ram**, **and brake his two horns**: and there was no power in the ram to stand before him, but he cast him down to the ground, and stamped upon him: and there was none that could deliver the ram out of his hand.

If you're impressed now, just wait, there's more....It seems that Daniel was given the *interpretation* to this vision at the end of Daniel 8, where he even mentions the players *by name* :

15 And it came to pass, when I, even I Daniel, had seen the vision, and sought for the meaning, then, behold, there stood before me as the appearance of a man.
16 And I heard a man's voice between the banks of Ulai, which called, and said, Gabriel, make this man to understand the vision.
17 So he came near where I stood: and when he came, I was afraid, and fell upon my face: but he said unto me, Understand, O son of man: for at the time of the end shall be the vision.
18 Now as he was speaking with me, I was in a deep sleep on my face toward the ground: but he touched me, and set me upright.
19 And he said, Behold, I will make thee know what shall be in the last end of the indignation: for at the time appointed the end shall be.
20 The ram which thou sawest having two horns are the kings of Media and Persia.
21 And **the rough goat is the king of Grecia: and the great horn that is between his eyes is the first king.**

Alexander the Great *was* this King of '**Grecia**!' and he *burned* through Asia Minor, Syria, Egypt, and Mesopotamia, and conquered every single territory from there to India in just twelve years. In the end, Alexander *easily* defeated **Media**, and Darius III of **Persia**, who had 500,000 soldiers, *with only 30,000 troops!* Remember, Daniel's vision came 250 years before this event had occurred.

Richards Topical Encyclopedia states the following :

Alexander's success was so extraordinary and his power so mighty that to many he must have seemed divinely inspired.

Before Alexander the Great, history had not witnessed conquest with the speed and accuracy with which this man subjugated the entire world. And Daniel's description of these events were uncanny.

Daniel had announced that when the 'he-goat' grew 'strong' (meaning, at the height of his power), the horn would be broken and in its place 'four notable horns would arise.' When Alexander was on his death bed he was asked, *'who will take over?'* To which Alex simply replied, *'the strongest'*; and that is exactly what happened. Fulfilling the prophecy to the letter, Alexander's great kingdom was divided between four of his generals after the empire's strongest figures all duked it out over the throne: *Cassander*, *Ptolemy*, *Antigonus*, and *Seleucus*. Look at the prophecy below being fulfilled in Daniel 8 :

King James Version (KJV)
8 Therefore **the he goat waxed very *great*: and when he was strong, the *great* horn was broken**; ***and for it came up four notable ones*** toward the four winds of heaven.

Calanus, a Hindu priest, accompanied Alexander and his Greek army on their conquests; the old spiritual guide was in his early seventies at that time. When the harsh conditions of the brutal trip fatigued the old monk, he informed Alexander that he would prefer death over living with a disability. So the monk chose death by **self-immolation**; *sacrificing himself* *to his idol Shiva—which is Hindi for 'the destroyer.'* Alexander attempted to change the mind of the old spiritual guide but he just couldn't persuade the old man.

A funeral pyre was built by Ptolemy. The pyre was then lit and, *reportedly*, the old monk didn't even grimace as he burnt with Alexander's powerful army looking-on in absolute disbelief. Before the pyre was lit and he burned alive, his last words to Alexander were '*We shall meet in Babylon.*'

History reports that Alexander wished to make Babylon the *capitol* of his empire but, after dying suddenly *in Babylon*, his dreams were dashed. Unbelievably, Alexander actually died *in* king Nebuchadnezzar's old throne room. It is clear that the death of Alexander, having died at only 32 years old, was the result of foul play—many toxicologists agree that Alexander's symptoms before passing away indicate poisoning.

The Bible even predicted that Alexander would die without a known cause —*perhaps from 'poisoning'*—when Daniel 8 went on to say :

> **25** And through his policy also he shall cause craft to prosper in his hand; and he shall magnify himself in his heart, and by peace [subversion] shall destroy many: **he shall also stand up against the Prince of princes; but he shall be broken without hand.**

Having been educated by the philosopher *Aristotle*, my guess is that Alexander was born, raised, and groomed, as a dupe savior who simply fulfilled a series of events that had been scripted for him long before his reign, *and, most likely, even before he was born*. The Hindu priest who sacrificed himself to 'the gods' by burning himself alive must certainly have been in on the whole plan to extinguish the 'great' warrior after Alexander's mission was accomplished; this would explain the appearance of a fulfilled prophecy when Alexander died suddenly, *after* the Hindu monk *Calanus's* last words, '*We shall meet in Babylon.*' This puzzling last utterance demonstrates that the Hindu Monks had been planning on sacrificing Alex too after his despotic purpose had been fulfilled.

You see, Alexander *had* to die in Nebuchadnezzar's throne room, because the establishment of *Babylon* as his world headquarters was contradictory to what **Isaiah** wrote in the Prophetic Scriptures. Isaiah 13 :

> King James Version (KJV)
> **19 And Babylon, the glory of kingdoms, the beauty of the Chaldees' excellency, shall be as when God overthrew Sodom and Gomorrah.**
> **20 It shall never be inhabited, neither shall it be dwelt in from generation to generation**: neither shall the Arabian pitch tent there; neither shall the shepherds make their fold there.
> 21 But wild beasts of the desert shall lie there; and their houses shall be full of doleful creatures; and owls shall dwell there, and satyrs shall dance there.
> 22 And the wild beasts of the islands shall cry in their desolate houses, and dragons in their * **pleasant palaces**: and her time is near to come, **and her days shall not be prolonged**.

In the following years, the desert slowly overtook the many millions of mud bricks which made up Babylon's crumbling buildings. The Shifting sands completely enveloped the entire infrastructure and eventually it was completely covered by the desert.

Saddam Hussein mistakenly thought that he too would rebuild the crumbled empire of Babylon in spite of the Prophetic Writings and you see how that turned out for him. **Saddam had even gone as far as building himself a *palace, fulfilling another prophecy in the last passage**, there which still sits empty to this day. Saddam *also* reportedly planned to build the ruins into a theme park and he even issued coins which featured his visage next to that of king Nebuchadnezzar of Babylon.

The ancient ruins of Babylon had been covered by the sands of time for thousands of years when the site garnered the attention of the terrible *East India Company (much more on this later)*. In 1792, the East India Company stepped up the dig to 'acquire Mesopotamian relics for shipment to London.'

Then in the 1900s, archaeologists digging in ancient Babylon discovered the terrible *Ishtar Gate*. Ishtar Gate was constructed into the north side of the main city wall by order of *King Nebuchadnezzar II—Biblical King Nebuchadnezzar's father*. As it was excavated, the bricks and pieces were sent to Berlin and rebuilt in the Pergamon Museum. The sinister project was completed in 1930, and now you too can behold the famous gates that Daniel must've passed through during his exile of Jerusalem if you fly to Germany.

I cannot help but notice that the year that the Ishtar Gate was rebuilt in **Germany—1930**—corresponds perfectly with the Babylonian antichrist climate which was heating up in the same *pre*-Nazi era. That the Ishtar Gate was moved to Germany and placed in the *****Pergamon** Museum* coincides with yet another scripture from Revelation 2, in which John condemns the *'church in **Pergamos**'*:

> **Revelation King James Version (KJV)**
> 12 And to the angel of the church in ***Pergamos** write; These things saith *he which hath the sharp sword with two edges (Yeshua!)*;
> 13 **I know thy works, and where thou dwellest, even where Satan's seat is**: and thou holdest fast my name, and hast not denied my faith, even in those days wherein Antipas was my faithful martyr, who was slain among you, **where Satan dwelleth**.

In the verse above, Jesus himself solidifies the fact that, 'satan's seat' too was moved to Germany from Ancient Rome just in time for the anti-christian climate of Nazi Germany, and to this day the infamous Ishtar Gate stands underneath the same roof. This really brings into question whether something *more* was discovered there—*something spiritual*. Revelation ***9...*** :

> King James Version (KJV)
> **13** And the sixth angel sounded, and I heard a voice from the four horns of the golden altar which is before God,

14 Saying to the sixth angel which had the trumpet, **Loose the four angels which are bound in *the great river Euphrates**.
15 And the four angels were *loosed*, which were prepared for an hour, and a day, and a month, and a year, **for to slay the third part of men**.

Note: The Ishtar gate was located right along ***the Great River Euphrates**.

These 'archaeologists' must have discovered the ancient remains of the ruling class of Babylon and perhaps their ancient bones were used as spiritual conduit to revive the spirits which possessed the wicked Babylon kings. I mean, within ten years after they moved Nebuchadnezzar's Ishtar Gate to Germany, *Germany too* were throwing **millions** of *their* neighbors into 'hot fiery' furnaces; *just like Nebuchadnezzar did to Daniel's pals!* Wow! Where did my preacher go to school? Yale?

Let us not forget that Hitler himself belonged to the German chapter of the nefarious fraternity of *The Order of Skull and Bones—Totenkopf, meaning 'dead head.'* The running story of the founding of *The Order of Skull and Bones,* Chapter 3:22 in Connecticut, cites that the German Chapter of their *'Order'* is *where William Huntington Russell* learned the ways of the *'Totenkopf.'*

I could go on-and-on about the prophecies surrounding these events since there are literally **thousands**, but the speed at which these events can be understood is the key to understanding The Bible as a whole.

However, I would like to share one final prophecy about Alexander the Great...

The *City of Tyre* was another *Phoenician* society which was not much different from Manhattan; *Tyre* was an incredible hub for shipping trade so it was a coveted stronghold for anyone vying for world dominion. *Ezekiel* not only predicted the first demise of Tyre, he predicted the second destruction of the city after it was moved to the island in the harbor of the old city, where it was incredibly fortified.

Nebuchadnezzar filled the prophecy of the destruction of Tyre, below, after which Alex the Great fulfilled a *third* prophecy written in verse 12. Ezekiel 26 :

11 With the hoofs of his horses shall he tread down all thy streets: he shall slay thy people by the sword, and thy strong garrisons shall go down to the ground.
12 And they shall make a spoil of thy riches, and make a prey of thy merchandise: and **they shall break down thy walls, and destroy thy pleasant houses: and they shall lay thy stones and thy timber and thy dust in the midst of the water.**

After Nebuchadnezzar leveled the City of Tyre in the prophecy above, the City was moved to an island in the *bay* across from the old city, presumably to prevent another predicted siege. Upon *Alexander's* siege of this new island version of Tyre, he did so by using the remains of the *old* City of Tyre which *Nebuchadnezzar* had prophetically destroyed; Alex cleverly commanded his soldiers to build a bridge by 'laying' the debris from Nebuchadnezzar's mess in the 'midst of the water!' And then, Alexander and his troops simply galloped upon the debris of the old city, *over the harbor*, and easily conquered the new island City of Tyre, just as Ezekiel had predicted. Goosebumps?

Rome's takeover of the Greco empire is not as easily quantified. It seems that the takeover of the Greek empire was terribly disorganized, sporadic, and a highly subversive process which spanned several centuries so, we won't attempt to explain it all. In the final chapters, we will learn more about the beginning of the Roman empire when we study the parallels between the 'literary' birth of Rome and the birth of America. And, though being 'not as easily quantified,' this empirical birth too was predicted by Daniel.

24. Dead Sea Scrolls

I know what you're thinking, and it is perfectly logical....*Many* men have posed the same question : How do we know that all of these prophecies weren't just scribbled down immediately following the events, and found millennia later? One simple answer : *The Dead Sea Scrolls!*

All of the Men of God who we have up till now called 'Prophets' *are Prophets* by divine providence; by a perfect, all-knowing God—*in the words of Daniel:* We have a God who changes the times and the seasons; He removes kings and makes kings; He imparts wisdom unto those who seek it, and knowledge to those who seek knowledge. He knows what is in the darkness, and the light dwells within Him; and now, YHWH reveals the deeply secret things :

Prophetically, at almost exactly the same moment in world history, *in 1948,* 'Israel' becomes a State *causing the 'Jews' to once again reoccupy the Holy Land*, and a young 'shepherd boy' casts a stone in a cave while looking for a lost member of his herd.

The young shepherd boy was wandering around the cliffs near the Dead Sea and when he tossed that fateful rock in the cave, he heard the echoing sound of pottery shattering. Upon examination, he discovered some ancient documents. Having not a clue what he'd found, the boy sold the dusty scrolls in town for a few bucks and after a long and sorted journey, nearly all of the documents ended up in one place, *mostly intact.*

Ha...A shepherd boy! In 1948? What a sense of humor YHWH has...

Nearly nine hundred separate scrolls were found but several, in particular, were extremely valuable from a historical point of view. There were two ancient copies of Daniel in the hoard! This proves that everything you just read about Daniel and Nebuchadnezzar, and Alexander the Great, *is all true.* You see, **all** of the *Old Testament,* save for the book of Esther, *were sealed in this ancient library—twice The Isaiah Scroll which was found relatively intact, is 1000 years older than any previously known copy of Isaiah!* The Book of Isaiah predicts the coming of the Messiah with great accuracy, *repeatedly!* He even tells us that Yeshua will come from 'the root of Jessie'—*King David's* father! He was right!

The book of Ezekiel, which was also in the Dead Sea Scroll hoard, is the prophetic document which predicted the following of the city of 'Tyre' : **'they shall lay thy stones and thy timber and thy dust in the midst of the water,'** after which Alexander the Great did exactly that. The details surrounding Ezekiel's prophecies, alone, could fill volumes.

The Book of Psalms foretells the account of the crucifixion of Christ in as much detail as the Gospel accounts themselves, long before the events took place. If you would like to take an adventure of discovery on your own, *read 22 Psalms;* we've all heard of the famous 23rd Psalms but 22

Psalms actually foretells the *words* of Yeshua as he hung on the cross, when Yeshua famously stated, 'My God, my God, why hast thou forsaken me?' As you read 22 Psalms, I would like for you to remember that Psalms was a Book of Songs written mostly by David, *long before these events.*

David was very musical and my favorite story about David—one which makes me smile from ear-to-ear—is the account in which David finally brought the Ark of the Lord into the City of David 'with gladness.' And as David and his band played their instruments and praised YHWH: '... *David danced before the Lord with all his might...*' It is easy to see why this handsome man, who was extremely musical, and a great warrior, was so beloved by both YHWH and his people.

As aforementioned, the Book of Psalms was a collection of inspirational songs written *mostly* by David; these songs were sung by the Twelve Tribes as they marched to aid YHWH in the extermination of the baby killers in Canaan, *long before* the *Psalm's prophecy of the birth and death of Christ was fulfilled.* The Dead Sea Scrolls included at least two copies the Book of Psalms which proves its provenance beyond any question!

The Old Testament alone consists of thousands of prophecies—nearly 30% of The Bible is prophecy—most of which pertained to the coming of the Messiah and *all* of those prophecies have already come to pass, *with flawless accuracy.* And the Dead Sea Scrolls were, unquestionably, sealed inside the jars in that cave for well over two thousand years. This lays to rest *any* questions as to The Bible's provenance.

Though dating proved them to be much older, the Scrolls are known to have been sealed in the caves, overlooking the Dead Sea, in or around 66 *AD*. The *Essenes*, a semitic group who were mentioned by Josephus and a few other sources, are the ancient group who hid the Scrolls. The Essenes observed the *Old Testament*. They believed in a *Messiah;* they practiced baptism; *they believed in a forthcoming apocalypse and a new covenant*. They were literally *Jews* turning into *Christians* at the same exact time *Christ* was being *baptized!*

The Essenes were being instructed in the ways of *'righteousness'* by one whom they referred to *as…*the *'Teacher of Righteousness.'* This, *'Teacher of Righteousness'* **was 'opposed and most likely killed by the establishment priesthood in Jerusalem.'** The enemies of this group were referred to as the *'Sons of Darkness'* but referred to *themselves* as the *'Sons of Light,'* *'the poor,'* and members of *'the Way.'* These are all names which were being counterfeited, *step-by-step,* from *Yeshua* as He walked the earth.

The good guys, *the Essenes*, were thought to be among the *good* Priesthood at the Temple in Jerusalem, but they were forced to evacuate because of the terror which these 'Sons of Darkness' wielded. The belief that this sect had pertained to the Temple was due to the fact that: A. Their library was so extensive and, B. They were in possession of a Copper Scroll which was discovered in Cave 3. This scroll records 64 places where ***treasure*** was buried; **the treasures are believed to be from the**

Temple in Jerusalem which were hidden away for safekeeping. One of the scrolls was actually titled: *The Temple Scroll.*

So here we have what must be an early version of the *Knights Templar,* a thousand years before their appearance *as,* 'The Knights Templar,' scoping out the Temple just before Christ was pursued and crucified by the Jewish Priesthood and the Romans, and there was a 'teacher of righteousness' living among the Essenes who was pursued and killed by the Romans? Oh….I almost forgot….There was also the copper scroll which was a treasure map of golden treasures from the Temple. Are we paying attention?

A museum has been placed in Jerusalem in which many of the scrolls are displayed today; the building is white and it was designed in the form of the clay jars in which the Scrolls were discovered—the white color of the building is said to represent the *real* '*Sons of Light,*' *the Essenes*. What is disturbing, though, is that whoever designed the monument also built a monument right in front of the giant clay-jar-building: this *other* 'monument' is an imposing, *black* wall which represents the '*Sons of Darkness.*'

25. Daniel and the Ishtar Gate

What I am about to tell you is utterly *amazing*, and you and I *must* be some of the very first people on earth to put these things altogether. Since the Ishtar gate was covered under a mountain of dirt for more than two thousand years, the things I am about to share with you would've been completely dark to history from *Daniel's Biblical times* to the times in which you and I now live today.

We will start out with another passage from our beloved Daniel; below is a vision which Daniel beheld about the end times and it corresponds with the things John wrote about in Revelation. Don't kill yourself trying to understand the meaning of this passage, for this read-through, because I only wish to point to the symbolism here. Daniel 7 :

> King James Version (KJV)
> **1** In the first year of Belshazzar king of Babylon Daniel had a dream and visions of his head upon his bed: then he wrote the dream, and told the sum of the matters.
> **2** Daniel spake and said, **I saw in my vision by night**, and, behold, the four winds of the heaven strove upon the great sea.
> **3 And four great beasts came up from the sea**, diverse one from another.

4 The first was like a lion, and had eagle's wings: I beheld till the wings thereof were plucked, and it was lifted up from the earth, and made stand upon the feet as a man...

When Daniel was exiled from his beloved Jerusalem and marched through the gates of Babylon, by king Nebuchadnezzar, he would've certainly taken notice of the glimmering-blue *Ishtar Gate*.

The Ishtar gate was covered in dragons, bulls, and *lions*. **These 'lions' all had 'eagles wings'** just as the one described in Daniel's 'night vision,' above. Are you ready to have your mind blown? Well, having studied the symbology of so many things pertaining to subjects from archaeology to road signs, I remembered the heraldry on the crest of arms for the royal family of Britain as I was reading verse 14 above. (You should google image the *royal coat of arms* now; you should also google image the keywords: *Ishtar Gate lion with eagle's wings*.)

What I found as I first gazed upon the crest was dumbfounding. There I beheld exactly what Daniel was pointing to from thousands of years in the past; in the passage, Daniel said: **'The first was like a lion, and had eagle's wings: I beheld till the wings thereof were plucked, and it was lifted up from the earth, and made stand upon the feet as a man.'**

As you look upon the image of the royal family crest, you will see a **'lion, whose wings have been plucked,' 'lifted from earth and standing on his hind feet as a man.'** Since this imagery had been buried for over two thousand years, this is an incredible Revelation!

Thousands of years preceding the design of the heraldry on the royal crest, Daniel *knew* that the Babylonian 'lion' with 'eagle's wings' would lose its wings and stand up on its hind legs; Daniel *too* seems to be pointing, blatantly, at the 'royal' family, as the headquarters of the 'MYSTERY BABYLON THE GREAT.'

What's more... As I read the book of Job, I discovered the meaning behind the *other* animal standing to the *right* side on the royal crest: There stands a unicorn which has been chained to the ground by a band. Below is a verse from the Book of Job, chapter 39 :

> King James Version (KJV)
> **9** Will the **unicorn** be willing to serve thee, or abide by thy crib?
> **10 Canst thou bind the unicorn with his *band* in the *furrow*?** or will he harrow the valleys after thee?

In The Bible, the *unicorn* has been used as a metaphor for God. I am not going to attempt to explain the meaning of the passage above; *that* I will leave as homework for you. I would just like to garner your attention to the fact that this *is* the exact same imagery which is illustrated on the *right* side of the royal family crest.

Here is the disturbing part: Save for the King James Version, nearly every subsequent translation of The Bible has been changed in order to remove this imagery from *The Bible*, rather than simply removing the unicorn from *their* family crest. The following are several translations of Job 39:10, in which the unicorn imagery has been removed to throw you from the scent trail of the royal family being *Hebrew* kings :

New International Version
Can you hold it [**ox**] to the furrow with a harness? Will it till the valleys behind you?

New Living Translation
Can you hitch a wild **ox** to a plow? Will it plow a field for you?

New American Standard Bible
Can you bind the wild **ox** in a furrow with ropes, Or will he harrow the valleys after you?

Holman Christian Standard Bible
Can you hold the wild **ox** to a furrow by its harness? Will it plow the valleys behind you?

International Standard Version
Can you bind the **ox** to plow a furrow with a rope? Will he harrow after you in the valley?

NET Bible
Can you bind the wild **ox** to a furrow with its rope, will it till the valleys, following after you?

New Heart English Bible
Can you hold the wild **ox** in the furrow with his harness? Or will he till the valleys after you?

Somehow, the royal family has removed the unicorn imagery from nearly every one of countless 'translations' of The Bible; this speaks to the awesome and widespread influence that this family still has on the entire world. This is also why you cannot trust any version save for the King James Version of The Bible.

Another troubling verse in the KJV of The Bible which *glares* at the 'royal' family is, the one in which The Book tells us that King David of the Tribe of Judah was a red-headed white boy. Enjoy this interesting observation of David which was made by the Palestinian giant, *Goliath.* I Samuel 17 :

King James Version (KJV)
42 And when the Philistine looked about, and saw David, he disdained him: for he was but a youth, and **ruddy**, and of a **fair countenance**. Merriam-Webster:

definition 1 :
having a healthy reddish color

The term 'Ruddy' in old times was used to describe someone having *'red hair.' Some* dictionaries now explain 'ruddy' to mean red face but, again, *it's more skullduggery.* The older dictionaries are all very clear about this definition. Below are the variances to which the above passage has been changed in subsequent translations of The Bible :

Holman Christian Standard Bible
When the Philistine looked and saw David, he despised him because **he was just a youth, healthy and handsome.**

International Standard Version
When the Philistine looked and saw David, he had contempt for him, because he was only a young man. **David had** a **dark, healthy complexion** [?] and was handsome.

GOD'S WORD® Translation
When the Philistine got a good look at David, he despised him. After all, David was a young man **with a healthy complexion and good looks**.

So, *see?* King David *was* a red-headed white boy—the fact has intentionally been hidden from you—and now if you google image a picture of *prince Harry*, the truth hidden behind the abstract screen of lies covering our world will come into a little better focus.

The throne upon which the British royals are all crowned is *called* the 'Throne of David' ; the *Harp* on their royal crest is designed to represent the account when David lovingly played his harp for King Saul, to calm the spirit with which the king was ***demon possessed!***

We also cannot lose sight of the fact that *all* of the US presidents are in bloodline with the royal family, and the presidential retreat is *called* 'Camp David.' And now *you* say: 'Dwight D. Eisenhower, named the retreat in honor of his father and grandson, both named David.' To which, I then say: How does the fact that his whole family has been named *David disprove my point?*

And even more damnatory: The same **star** imagery that appears on the **Ishtar Gate**—*the main gate of Babylon*—is *also* featured on the British **Union Jack flag.** The star means 'god' in *cuneiform*—again, *Babylonian*. (Cuneiform is the oldest known language in the world! This is more proof that the Tower of Babel account is the true origin of civilization!) That's not all! The *'Jack'* in Union **Jac**k stands for '**Jacob**,' on which the 12 points of the star of Ishtar represent the *re-**union** of the Twelve Tribes of **Jac**ob.*

The Babylonian word for 'god' has also been scribed on the ground surrounding the giant obelisk which stands at the center of Vatican Square! To see this for yourself, google image an aerial view of Vatican Square. The 'obelisk' is a representation of the sun 'god' himself; many ancient accounts point to this structure as being the 'lost penis of Osiris' who is the Egyptian version of King Nimrod (When you have time, you should read the story).

The giant obelisk in Saint Peter's Square is ancient Egyptian in origin, and was moved all the way to Italy by the disgusting Roman Emperor, *Caligula, 2000 years ago*. The revolting statue was brought 2400-odd miles for an attraction as the centerpiece for the *'Circus of Caligula'* which was the public venue where the Apostles Peter and Paul were publicly sacrificed. The *Circus of Caligula* was also known as the 'Circus of Nero'; it was a spot where you would take the family on a Sunday, to watch the Apostles and followers of Yeshua lose their lives in the most disgusting ways man could imagine.

The obelisk which was the centerpiece of the Roman 'circus' of terror, and which witnessed the spilled blood of so many of Yeshua's followers, was *so* important to the *Roman Catholic Church* that, in 1586, *pope Sixtus V* ordered to have the obelisk moved just a few hundred meters to its present location, in front of the construction site of the new *St. Peter Basilica*. You heard right, the title deed to the public venue where the Saints, including the Apostles Paul and Peter, were slaughtered, never even changed hands when the Roman Emperor's morphed into their new roles as 'the gods'; only in this case they referred to themselves as: 'Popes.'

You see, the system of antichrist was completely ripe when Jesus and his beloved followers all began to witness the inevitable implosion of Rome, and Christianity was making its beautiful genesis in the dark side's black wake. Below, Revelation speaks on the topic of being 'drunken with the blood of the saints.' Revelation 17 :

> King James Version (KJV)
> **6 And I saw the *woman* drunken with the blood of the *saints*, and with the blood of the martyrs of Jesus**: and when I saw her, I wondered with great admiration.

Ishtar—the *original* 'Whore of Babylon' was a *female* 'goddess!' When you combine the facts that, the Babylonian word for 'god' is written on the ground surrounding this giant representation of King Nimrod's penis, in front of which **Saint** Paul and **Saint** Peter were killed, and Caligula being the Roman emperor who moved the penis there in the first place, this *all* becomes very concerning. I think we may have solved the 'mystery' spoken-of by John of Revelation 17 :

> King James Version (KJV)
>
> 4 And the **woman was arrayed in** *purple* **and** *scarlet* colour, and decked with gold and precious stones and pearls, having a golden cup in her hand full of abominations and filthiness of her fornication:
>
> 5 And upon her forehead was a name written, **Mystery, Babylon The Great,** The **Mother Of Harlots And Abominations Of The Earth**.

Only queens and kings, *during John's times*, dressed in '**purple and scarlet**.' With the advent of the Roman Catholic Church, the clergy followed suit in the adornment of these colors.

26. King of Kings

A cousin of prince William's who will go unnamed, *and who seems to be a Christian*, did us all the huge favor of tracing their ancestry *all the way back to Adam and Eve*. When I was young, I would read those pages-and-pages of so-and-so begat so-and-so and wonder: *why on earth would YHWH include all of this in The Bible? Now*, I know! Enjoy :

YHWH

Adam and Eve (B. C. 4000-3070)

1. Seth (B. C. 3869-2957)

2. Enos (B. C. 3764-2859)

3. Canaan (B. C. 3674-2895)

4. Mahalaleel (B. C. 3604-2709)

5. Jared (B. C. 3539-2577)

6. Enoch (B. C. 3377-3012)

7. Methusaleh (B. C. 3312-2344)

8. Lamech (B. C. 3125-2349)

9. **Noah** (B. C. 2943-2007), Naamah

10. Shem (B. C. 2441-1841)

11. Arphaxad (B. C.2341-1903)

12. Salah (B. C.2306-1873)

13. Heber (B. C. 2276-181)

14. Peleg (B. C. 2241-2003)
15. Reu (B. C. 2212-1973)
16. Serug (B. C. 2180-2049)
17. Nahor (B. C. 2050-2002)
18. Terah (B. C. 2221-1992), Amtheta
19. **Abraham** (B. C. 1992-1817), **Sarah**
20. **Isaac** (B. C. 1896-1716), Rebekah
21. **Jacob** (B. C. 1837-1690), Leah
22. **Judah** (b. B. C. 1752), Tamar
23. Pharez
24. Hezron
25. Aram
26. Aminadab
27. Naasson
28. Salmon
29. Boaz (B. C. 1312), Ruth
30. Obed
31. Jesse

Kings of Judah

32. **King David** (B. C. 1085-1015), Bathsheba
33. **King Solomon** (B. C. 1033-975), Naamah
34. King Rehoboam (b. B. C. 1016, d. 958), Maacah
35. King Abijah (B. C. 958-955)
36. King Asa (B. C. 955-914), Azubah
37. King Jehoshaphat (B. C. 914-889)
38. **King Jehoram** (B. C. 889-885), Athaliah

39. King Ahaziah (B. C. 906-884), Zibiah
40. King Joash (B. C. 885-839), Jehoaddan
41. King Amaziah (b. B. C. 864, d. 810), Jecholiah
42. King **Uzziah** (b. B. C. 826, d. 758), Jerusha
43. King Jotham (b. B. C. 783, d. 742)
44. King Ahaz (b. B. C. 787, d. 726), Abi
45. **King Hezekiah** (b. B. C. 751, d. 698), Hephzibah
46. King Manasseh (b. B. C. 710, d. 643), Meshullemeth
47. King Amon (b. B. C. 621, d. 641), Jedidiah
48. King Josiah (b. B. C. 649, d. 610), Mamutah
49. King Zedekiah (B. C. 599-578)

Kings of Ireland
50. Queen Tea Tephi (b. B. C. 565), marries Eochaidh, a Prince of the scarlet thread, later King Heremon, descended from Zerah
51. King Irial Faidh (reigned 10 years)
52. King Eithriall (reigned 20 years)
53. Follain
54. King Tighernmas (reigned 50 years)
55. Eanbotha
56. Smiorguil
57. King Fiachadh Labhriane (reigned 24 years)
58. King Aongus Ollmuchaidh (reigned 21 years)
59. Maoin
60. King Rotheachta (reigned 25 years)
61. Dein
62. King Siorna Saoghalach (reigned 21 years)

63. Oholla Olchaoin

64. King Giallchadh (reigned 9 years)

65. King Aodhain Glas (reigned 20 years)

66. King Simeon Breac (reigned 7 years)

67. King Muirteadach Bolgrach (reigned 4 years)

68. King Fiachadh Toigrach (reigned 7 years)

69. King Duach Laidhrach (reigned 10 years)

70. Eochaidh Buailgllerg

71. King Ugaine More the Great (reigned 30 years)

72. King Cobhthach Coalbreag (reigned 30 years)

73. Meilage

74. King Jaran Gleofathach (reigned 7 years)

75. King Coula Cruaidh Cealgach (reigned 25 years)

76. King Oiliolla Caisfhiachach (reigned 28 years)

77. King Eochaidh Foltleathan (reigned 11 years)

78. King Aongns Tuirmheach Teamharch (reigned 30 years)

79. King Eana Aighneach (reigned 28 years)

80. Labhra Suire

81. Blathucha

82. Easamhuin Famhua

83. Roighnein Ruadh

84. Finlogha

85. Fian

86. King Eodchaidh Feidhlioch (reigned 12 years)

87. Fineamhuas

88. King Lughaidh Raidhdearg

89. King Criomhthan Niadhnar (reigned 16 years)

90. Fearaidhach Fion Feachtnuigh

91. King Fiachadh Fionoluidh (reigned 20 years)

92. King Tuathal Teachtmar (reigned 40 years)

93. King Coun Ceadchathach (reigned 20 years)

94. King Arb Aonflier (reigned 30 years)

95. King Cormae Usada (reigned 40 years)

96. King Caibre Liffeachair (reigned 27 years)

97. King Fiachadh Sreabthuine (reigned 30 years)

98. King Muireadhach Tireach (reigned 30 years)

99. King Eochaidh Moigmeodhin (reigned 7 years)

100. King Nail of the **Nine** Hostages

101. Eogan

102. K. Murireadhach

103. Earca

Kings of Argyleshire

104. King Fergus More

105. King Dongard

106. King Conran

107. King Aidan (d. 604)

108. King Eugene IV. (d. 622)

109. King **Donald** IV. (d. 650)

110. Dongard

111. King Eugene. V. (d. 692)

112. Findan

113. King Eugene VII. (d. A. D. 721), Spondan

114. K. Etfinus (d. A. D. 761), Fergina

115. King Achaius (d. A. D. 819), Fergusia
116. King Alpin (d. A. D. 834)

Kings of Scotland

117. King Kenneth I (842-858)
118. King Constantin I (862-876)
119. King Donald II (889-900)
120. King Malcolm I (943-954)
121. King Kenneth II (971-995, d. A. D. 995)
122. King Malcolm II (1005-1034, d. A. D. 1034)
123. Bethoc, married to Crinan, Mormaer of Atholl and lay abott of Dunkeld
124. King Duncan I (1034-1040, d. A. D. 1040), Sibyl
125. King Malcolm III Canmore (A. D. 1058-1093), Margaret of England
126. King David I (1124-1153, d. A. D. 1153), Matilda of Huntingdon
127. Prince Henry (d. A. D. 1152), Ada of Surrey
128. Earl David of Huntingdon (d. A. D. 1219), Matilda of Chester
129. Isobel m. Robert Bruce III
130. Robert Bruce IV. m. Isobel of Gloucester
131. Robert Bruce V. m. Martha of Carrick
132. King Robert I (The Bruce) (A. D. 1306-1329), Isobel, daughter of Earl of Mar
133. Marjorie Bruce m. Walter Stewart III
134. K. Robert II (b. 1317, 1371-1390, d. A. D. 1390), Euphemia of Ross (d. A. D. 1376)
135. K. Robert III. (b. 1337, 1390-1406, d. A. D. 1406), Annabella Drummond (d. A. D. 1401)

136. King James I of Scotland (A. D. 1406-1437), (16g grandson of King Alfred The Great) m. Joan Beaufort

137. King James II of Scotland M. Mary of Gueldres

138. King James III of Scotland m. Margaret Princess of Denmark

139. King James IV of Scotland (b. 1473, 1488-1513, d. A. D. 1543), Margaret of England (d. A. D. 1539)

140. King James V of Scotland. (b. 1513, 1513-1542, d. A. D. 1542), Mary of Lorraine (d. A. D. 1560)

141. Queen Mary (also known as Mary, Queen of Scots) (b. 1542, 1542-1567, d. A. D. 1587), Lord Henry Darnley (d. 1567). (Mary became Queen when she was just six days old. She was deposed as Queen in 1567 and was executed in 1587)

142. King James VI. and I. (A. D. 1603-1625), Ann of Denmark. James became James I of England (A. D. 1603-1625) in 1603 while still King James VI of Scotland

143. Princess Elizabeth (d. 1662), Frederick V, Elector Palatine

144. Princess Sophia, (d. 1714), m. Duke Ernest of Brunswick (d. 1698)

145. King George I. (1714-1727), Sophia Dorothea of Zelle (1667-1726)

146. King George II. (b. 1683, 1727-1760), Princess Caroline of Brandenburg-Anspach (1683-1737)

147. Prince Frederick Lewis of Wales (1707-1751), Princess Augusta of Saxe-Gotha-Altenberg

148. King George III (b. 1738, 1760-1820), Princess Sophia of Mecklenburgh-Strelitz (1744-1818)

149. Duke Edward of Kent (1767-1820), Princess Victoria of Saxe-Coburg (d. 1861)

150. Queen Victoria (b. 1819, 1837-1901), Prince Albert of Saxe-Coburg & Gotha

151. King Edward VII. (b. 1841, 1901-1910), Princess Alexandra

152. King George V. (b. 1865, 1910-1936), Princess Mary

153. King George VI. (b. 1895, 1936-1952), Lady Elizabeth Bowes-Lyon (Queen Elizabeth, The Queen Mother) (b. 1900, d. 2002)

154. Queen Elizabeth II (b. 1926, reigned from 1952), Philip Duke of Edinburgh 156. Prince Charles of Wales (b. 1948) Princess Diana (d. 1997)

155. William, Duke of Cambridge (b. 1982) m. Catherine, Duchess of Cambridge (née Middleton)

156. Prince George Alexander Louis of Cambridge

Having always heard the rumors that the royal family was a modern evolution of The Biblical *House of David*, it is documented that Queen Victoria spent one million Pounds *proving* that her bloodline does in fact lead directly to Solomon through the Davidic bloodline; if you google image 'the royal lines from Zarah and Pharez Judah' you can view a chart which is the result of the Queen's chartered research.

> Note: Every one of Queen Victoria's nine children married into the thrones of neighboring countries which is another *powerful* example of YHWH's covenant with Abraham in Genesis 17.

The most amazing finding in Queen Victoria's chartered bloodline chart is, the branch of the royal bloodline in which Jesus is found. We all know that Jesus was, prophetically, stated to have come down through the Judah bloodline but here is what is fascinating: *Jesus* came down through the

Nathan side of the bloodline, not through the loins of Nathan's brother, *King Solomon*. *The Bible* even lists Nathan as one of the ancestors of Christ, in Luke 3:31. Nathan was Solomon's *righteous* brother, and it is not known if David's son and the Prophet during Solomon's reign were one-in-the-same! But, if so, this would be the *Nathan* who instructed David *'not'* to build the Temple.

The royal family takes great pride in the fact that *they* come from an unbroken line of kings and even that the 'King of Kings' came down through *their* bloodline. The fact that the 'Lion of Judah'—*the return of Christ*—will also come down through this same bloodline, paves the way for the one who will be called the 'antichrist' to come down through *British* royal blood *as well*. And, if Queen Victoria's purveyors of genealogy were right—and at the risk of their heads, *I am sure that they were*—*we all* have the Solomon branch of the bloodline of Yeshua running through *our own* veins. This proves, once again, that, *we are all Judah!*

Here is why: If you will remember, when King Solomon went bad, he began building Temples to Baal at which the ladies of the entire empire ritually burned their babies alive; *remember?* This is how Solomon ended up with '700 wives and 300 concubines.' And, if Solomon *had* permanently held on to that many women, imagine how many had become pregnant and were released back to their home lands! The funny thing about *this* is, the British throne is *so* proud of their 'royal' blood, but, in the end, we *all* have King Solomon's blood flowing through our veins!

This means that the evil mechanism of Solomon's lust is also the action which *fulfilled* the Abrahamic covenant which mingled with *all* of our seed (Genesis 12:3). In Hebrew, the Abrahamic covenant is described by the words: **brit** *milah*, which means: 'covenant of circumcision.' This is where the names, '**Brit**ain,' '**Brit**ish,' and '**Brit**,' *really* come from.

When Jacob, the Patriarch to the Twelve Tribes of Israel, was prophesying to his Twelve Sons concerning the fates of their individual tribes, he had the following to say about the Tribe of Judah. Genesis 49 :

> King James Version (KJV)
> 8 Judah, thou art he whom thy brethren shall praise: **thy hand shall be in the neck of thine enemies**; thy father's children shall bow down before thee.
> 9 **Judah is a lion's whelp**: from the prey, my son, **thou art gone up: he stooped down, he couched as a lion**, and as an old lion; **who shall rouse him up**?
> 10 **The sceptre shall not depart from Judah, nor a lawgiver from between his feet, until Shiloh come; and unto him shall the gathering of the people be**.
> 11 Binding his foal unto the vine, and his ass's colt unto the choice vine; **he washed his garments in wine, and his clothes in the blood of grapes**:
> 12 **His eyes shall be red with wine, and his teeth white with milk**.

So, above, in the very first Book of The Bible, we have Jacob telling his son Judah that not only would every king of the world come from Judah's loins—as we have already proven in this chapter—but the final King would also come from the Tribe of Judah; the King of Kings and Lord of Lord's: *Yeshua*!

I cannot even tell you how many times The Bible mentions the above promise but it's a *lot*. The 'British' 'Royal Family' are simply a modern evolution of a seamless Bible 'Story' which started in the Old Testament, initially with the ancient Kings of Judah. And, though this is the same Tribe which produced Christ himself, most of these evil, Hebrew Kings were *anything* but Christ-*like*.

Below is the account in Revelation describing the moment Yeshua comes back. I would like for you to notice that Jacob's prophecy of Yeshua **'washing his garments in wine, His clothes in the blood of grapes, His eyes shall be red with wine**, and his teeth white with milk,' is nearly identical from the first Book of the Bible to the last. Revelation 19 :

> King James Version (KJV):
> 11 And I saw heaven opened, and behold a white horse; and he that sat upon him was called Faithful and True, and in righteousness he doth judge and make war.
> **12 His eyes were as a flame of fire, and on his head were many crowns**; and he had a name written, that no man knew, but he himself.

13 And he was clothed with a vesture dipped in blood: and his name is called The Word of God.

14 And the armies which were in heaven followed him upon white horses, clothed in fine linen, white and clean.

15 And **out of his mouth goeth a sharp sword, that with it he should smite the nations**: and he shall rule them with a rod of iron: and he treadeth the winepress of the fierceness and wrath of Almighty God.

16 And he hath on his vesture and on his thigh a name written, King Of Kings, And Lord Of Lords.

Our ancient history was carefully preserved in order for God to warn us of the evil heirs of these Hebrew Kings who rule every nation, *still today*. Most of us will only recognize them as evil, sadly, when the horrors are already upon us and our families.

27. Where 'Iron' Meets 'Clay'

If you study the verse below, the fate of the poor slaves who built the Tower of Babel becomes very clear—it explains how all people including the 'American Indians' landed on separate continents. Genesis 11 :

> King James Version (KJV)
> **4** And they said, Go to, let us build us a city and a tower, whose top may reach unto heaven; and let us make us a name, **lest we be scattered abroad upon the face of the whole earth**.

It is made clear, in the verse above, by the use of the word 'lest' that these people were threatened. It appears that despite their slave-master's promises to *not* 'scatter' them 'abroad upon the face of the earth' or 'confuse' their 'language' *if they 'built'* this 'tower,' in the end, the offering of this great pyramid *didn't* please 'the gods'—*Nimrod*.

The passage below demonstrates that Nimrod *was* a great city builder. Genesis 10 :

> King James Version (KJV)
> **10** And the beginning of his kingdom was Babel, and Erech, and Accad, and Calneh, in the land of Shinar.

11 Out of that land went forth Asshur, and builded Nineveh, and the city Rehoboth, and Calah,
12 And Resen between Nineveh and Calah: the same is
13 And Mizraim begat Ludim, and Anamim, and Lehabim, and Naphtuhim,
14 And Pathrusim, and Casluhim, (out of whom came Philistim,) and Caphtorim.
15 And Canaan begat Sidon his first born, and Heth,
16 And the Jebusite, and the Amorite, and the Girgasite,
17 And the Hivite, and the Arkite, and the Sinite,

Now that we know that Nimrod was *very astute* at this real life SimsCity game, the only missing ingredient which one would need in order to build these cities *overseas was*, Nimrod's great granddad's **big *boat!*** The next scripture, below, picks up where we left off in Genesis Chapter 10, and actually names some of the Canaanite Tribes who were spread abroad to become 'Indians!' Again, Genesis 10 :

18 And the Arvadite, and the Zemarite, and the * **Hamathite: and afterward were the families of the Canaanites spread abroad.**

Note: * *Hematite* is the natural ore from which iron is refined.

The verse below shows where these tribes who were scattered to North America got their *bow* and arrow technology. 2 Samuel 1 :

King James Version (KJV)

18 (Also he bade them teach the children of Judah the use of the bow: behold, it is written in the book of Jasher. [Jasher is an ancient book which was lost ages ago])

A quick glance of the scriptures showing Nimrod's cities, above, will demonstrate why our forefathers were all *surveyors*, and why they founded this country under *separate* states. It is clear that the trap doors for evil were constructed right into the constitution when it speaks of a 'more perfect **union**.'

Note: Most people don't even realize that there were *Twelve* original companies who founded the corporation of the United States of America, *not 13* as we've wrongfully been informed; the thirteenth colony settled much later. The twelve colonies of the US were symbolic of the Twelve Tribes of Israel; this shows that these companies' royal founders *thought* they were forming the *New Jerusalem* spoken-of in *Revelation*.

Events like the Civil War and God himself knows whatever else they will do to us, wouldn't even be possible were it not for the 'Risk' board game structure of our map, and stacking us all in cities which were *designed* with the keys to their very destruction—'*Antithesis*'—in mind from day one. War is a necessary evil for the system of antichrist, *for many reasons*: war creates the illusion that we need these creeps for protection. It was also a major financial opportunity, as well as being a mechanism for 'thinning the heard'—*human sacrifice*.

Noah's great technology of moving biological creatures was retooled for transporting **man**, and trading his resources, which led to the 'famine' spoken-of in Revelation. We watched the evolution of this take place during more modern times when the East India Company's slave ships delivered millions of people to their new owners, in America and otherwise. This slavery technology is a high-tech evolution of the accounts recorded in Exodus.

We saw a modern evolution of this same technology when the steamers loaded with our relatives docked at Ellis Island. They were all moved with Noah's great technology which people scoffed-at generations earlier. So, I have a terrible time wondering how people can be so stiff-necked as to believe that Nimrod—*Noah's Great Grandson—couldn't* have delivered the 'Indians' to the Americas, ages ago on great boats. Especially when you see the ocean liners today.

If you just sit and watch the waterways from the top of '**One World**' Trade Center while eating at *Windows of the World* and meditating on this concept, you might just feel chill bumps racing down your neck.

Many tribes of the 'natives' of North America speak languages which are, no doubt, Hebrew dialects. Ancient, leather phylactery boxes have also been found in burial mounds on the continent.

East India Company was formed in 1600. In 1606—just six years later —'*The Virginia Company of London'* was formed as the first **British** joint-stock company created **with the intent of establishing a permanent**

settlement in the 'New' World. In their new corporation, the '*Virginia Company*,' the British ruling class carried on the traditional racial slur used for the people of India—'Indians'—to describe the 'Indians' of their 'New' World.

Yes, *Indian* is also what EIC clearing-agents called the 'Native Americans.' The first order of business in 'Virginia' was passing out smallpox infected blankets and handkerchiefs to the locals, to make room for the *new* throne-holders of the '*New* World.' It is estimated that millions of Native Americans were killed by disease alone in the 'smallpox giveaway program.'

It really isn't all that hard to understand why this was the empire that Daniel saw as 'iron mixed with clay.' The creeps who invaded this country, mainly from Spain, Britain, and France would have evolved from the Roman Empire which was indeed an Empire of Iron. And, if *you've* ever been to a 'Native' American museum, you know that literally everything they owned was made from *clay*.

Many of the directors of EIC married into the local royal gene pools, leaving nothing left of the physical appearance of the British people after a generation or two; the Bible speaks of this extensively. This Royal Hebrew bloodline conquered the whole world and sat at the thrones of all nations while they were at it.

All of the *Presidents* of the USA—*EIC's new corporation*—are blood relatives with the old Directors of East India Company; yes, *even Obama*.

These are the descendants of enterprising merchants, murderers, slavers, and *conquerers* of the known world which was all prophetically described, millennia prior, in the Holy Bible. They're the '**Merchants of the Earth**' spoken-of in Revelation 18 :

King James Version (KJV)
3 For **all nations** have drunk of the wine of the wrath of her fornication, and **the kings of the earth have committed fornication with her**, and the **merchants of the earth are waxed rich through the abundance of her delicacies**.

Afghanistan is now the new war-torn India. And American troops now guard opium fields for the sons of darkness, over there.

28. Constantine

New York City inherited her name from the ancient city of *York*. The Romans 'colonized' York in the same way that Britain had 'colonized' *New York*; meaning, there were *already* a metropolis of people living there, who were subjugated and forced to live under Roman rule, when *they* 'settled' *York*.

York became a strategic Roman foothold which passed from Roman to viking rule and finally fell into the hands of modern Britain through another viking king of the same bloodline, during *William the Conquerer's* swath of terror. York was *so* important to Rome that the Emperors *Hadrian, Septimius Severus,* and *Constantius I*, all held court in the city during their various campaigns.

During *his* stay in York, *after his father had died*, Constantine the Great was proclaimed Emperor by the troops stationed in York's fortress, *in 306 AD*. After being 'proclaimed' Emperor, Constantine quoted a long passage from the *Sibylline Oracles*; and, yes, this is the same 'Sibyl'—'prophetess-giant'—with which we started this journey (more on this soon). Skipping the long and sorted history of the events, *Constantine* is the Roman Emperor who invented the brilliant idea of calling emperors 'Popes.'

Christianity was banned by the Roman Empire for the first 280 years of Roman rule, during which period the Christians were terribly persecuted. The sensation that the vacuum of Christ in human form had caused, snowballed into a great Christian movement that had become more than troublesome for the Roman empire. Actually, that is a gross understatement. In the end, the message which was spread by this poor carpenter's son is the major contributing factor to the toppling of the powerful Roman empire.

Constantine 'envisioned' Christianity as a religion that could 'unite the Roman empire,' which at that time was beginning to fragment and divide as the incredible movement gained steam. Constantine then created a Roman fusion of 'Christianity' mixed with all of the old mystery religions and pagan practices which had evolved from ancient Babylon and, voila— *you have the Catholic Church!* So, in other words, Constantine was the genius who'd had the brilliant plan of instituting the old, *if you can't beat 'em - join 'em,* method.

If you think about it, this move was brilliant since, 'the gods' of Rome— *Emperors*—could *continue* being 'gods.' But this time 'the gods' would take *Christ's* place, *immediately following his physical absence,* after they, themselves, *killed* him. Just like Nimrod supposedly killed YHWH in the mountains; the popes are now all considered to be 'Christ Vicar' or, 'earthly representative of Christ.'

Just as with nearly every civilization since time began, Constantine was a sun worshiper before *and after* his supposed conversion to Christianity. In honor of the sun god, *Apollo—the destroyer of Revelation 9/11*—Constantine *forbade* the ancient Judaic tradition of resting on Saturday when he changed the day on which we honor the Sabbath to Sunday. Constantine then named the old Jewish Sabbath, *Saturn*-day, in honor of the sun god, saturn—Apollo's *old* name. To add insult to injury, he also named this new 'sabbath' after his pagan god when deeming the new day of rest: **Sun**-day. In doing so, Constantine single-handedly bastardized these ancient Judaic traditions by imposing these blasphemous rules upon the entire planet and we all still honor these pagan rituals today.

The order of the false prophet, *Catholicism*, pacified the Christian movement and had even crippled its power since the masses were now unknowingly duped into worshipping all of the deities from the past, on all of the wrong dates and days, in all of the wrong temples, and taking part in all of the pagan rituals and chants which had evolved from the ancient mystery religions of ancient Babylon. Constantine even changed the name of Christ, from the Hebrew name, *Yeshua,* to the Latin name, *Jesus*—which is pronounced: *Hey-Zeus! This is why this book refers to him by his Hebrew name.*

This is the abomination which had allowed the Roman empire to rule this 'New World Order' from the two legs of a new *fused* empire: the '*pope*' in Rome, and the *British empire*. This is the synthesis which has evolved into the illusion of a 'free world.' But this too is the same old Roman rule in different dress: men enslaving other men and parading around as 'the gods.' The Roman empire had no choice but to evolve and they did.

And perhaps one of the greatest tricks that this new Rome instituted was the 'two party' 'democracy'—*the illusion of choice.* And, how this old magic trick still persuades people to pick a voiceless dummy and relentlessly defend and promote 'their' political ideals to their family, blows my mind. Think of the absurdity of this: The 'vetting process' ensures that our only two choices are in bloodline with the royal family, and that their loyalty lines up with the ruling order's sick practices. We are then given only two choices from which to choose; these are literally the same odds as flipping a coin if things were on the square, but *their* coin has heads on both sides.

New York, itself—originally named *New Amsterdam*—was *also* a bustling metropolis of mud brick buildings, filled with rabbles of Native American people, when the 'pilgrims' arrived. They then filled the Island of manhattan with every manner of pyramid, skyscraper, tower and building, anyone could ever dream up.

The Biblical account of the very first **world** empire—*the Tower of Babel account*—is now coming to a conclusion. We once again speak the same language using *computer translators,* and are 'as one' in too many ways to count. Our technology too has now 'reached the heavens,' for the kings of this earth have 'killed God' and 'elevated' *themselves* to the same status as 'the gods.' From the kings of ancient Babylon to the Pharaohs to the Romans to the Viking kings to the Hebrew Kings and, finally, they are *all* in bloodline with the 'British Royal Family,' and they all believed to be 'the gods.'

We are in the very *twilight of truth*. For soon instead of 'book-burnings,' the internet will simply be switched off and we will be left with the same single truth that has survived the finality of spent time—*The Holy Bible*.

29. Human Sacrifice

Below are a long list of 'coincidences' surrounding the Las Vegas shooting, *which I believe cannot be ignored.*

1—**Stephen's** first name means '**crown**.'

1—The first name of the Security Guard who was supposedly shot in the leg while approaching the door of the gunman's suite, goes by the name '*Jesus*'—God in man form who is indeed the '*King of Kings*.' *Jesus*, being a King, **would hypothetically wear a** '*crown*'—**which is the meaning of Stephen's first name**.

2—According to dictionary.com, Steve's last name, *Paddock*, means :

> pad·dock ˈpadək/noun
>
> A small field or **enclosure where horses are kept or exercised**. synonyms: field, meadow, pasture;'

The oldest form of the name 'Apollo' is traced back to a Doric word, *apella* (ἀπέλλα), which originally meant '**fence for animals**.' So, the gunman's name literally translates to, *'the crowning of Apollo.'* Among other qualities, Apollo was considered the 'god of the herd,' and one major job of a shepherd is to 'cull,' *or,* 'thin,' his herd.

2—Jesus's last name is 'Campos,' or, '**grassy field**.' Which seems to mirror the meaning of Stephen **Paddock's** last name.

When Stephen **Paddock** gunned down dozens of people in Las Vegas, *he* 'culled' the herd from a *'tower'* at Mandalay Bay; *King Nimrod was the first 'king' to ever wear a crown and Nimrod was the inventor of the 'tower.'*

The *'paddock'* — *'grassy field' (security guard's surname)*—in which the victims were shot, **was positioned directly in front of a pyramid**—the *Luxor,* owned by **MGM** *Grand*—where, historically these types of sacrifices have been made, around the world, since the times of Nimrod *who built the very first pyramid.* Remember, also, that Peter and Paul—*the Apostles*—were killed beneath an obelisk where the Vatican now stands, and there was an obelisk in front of MGM's pyramid.

—The *'paddock'* in which these folks were murdered was sandwiched between *Russell Boulevard*—named for the evil family who founded *Skull and Bones*—and Mandalay's *Delano Tower,* a *tower* which was named after the dope-dealing *Warren Delano,* who was 'chief dope hustler' at Russell and Company (an American evolution of the dope-dealing East India Company). If you've read *Sacred Scroll of Seven Seals,* you already know that Warren Delano *is Franklin Delano Roosevelt's granddad.*

—The shooter fired from the 32nd floor—or 'level'—of said, 'tower.' The **masonic hierarchy pyramid** displaying the varying degrees of freemasonry *also, unbelievably,* **uses the image of a pyramid to demonstrate the 'degrees of freemasonry,'** which are a more complex and benign form of brainwashing than satanism.

If you google the *masonic hierarchy poster*, you will see that it shows a different guy dressed in all of the silly costumes and regalia of the group, standing upon key *steps* of the pyramid, with the corresponding 'degree' listed under the man on each step. At the apex of the *masonic hierarchy pyramid*, a Knights Templar is holding the right side of a banner while the 33rd degree freemason holds the other end of the banner, showing that the two are working in unison (*you should google it, it really is unbelievable*). Similarly, *Excalibur*—a medieval, knight-themed casino—stands next to MGM's pyramid, representing the freemasons' bond with the Knights Templar....*Excalibur is also owned my MGM.* **These casinos meet between the 3200 and 3300 blocks of Russell Boulevard!**

Remembering that Mr. Paddock shot from the **32nd floor**, below is the corresponding description for the **32nd degree of freemasonry**—the *step* just before the final 33 degree, which is the apex of the 'masonic hierarchy pyramid.' I won't single out a particular masonic lodge here, but, *just as with any of the statements herein*, a quick cut and paste into google will lead a person right to the provenance of this statement. Look :

"32° Sublime Prince of the Royal Secret. **This degree describes the victory of the spiritual over the human in man** and the conquest of appetites and passions by moral sense and reason. **The exemplar represents every Freemason eager to serve humanity but caught between self-interest and the call of duty. Duty often requires** *sacrifice*, **sometimes the** * *supreme sacrifice*.

Just to clear up any last confusion as to whether this *was* a human sacrifice, Yourdictionary.com defines this * **'supreme sacrifice'** as below :

> **'Supreme Sacrifice: Supreme sacrifice is defined as something a person would give their life for.** An example of a **supreme sacrifice is a soldier giving their life for their country.'**

The clever name of the concert event where this fiasco occurred was coined '*Route 91 Harvest* Festival.'

-The **Crown**—***king***—opened fire from the 32nd floor of a Tower, ***harvesting*** the concertgoers who were trapped inside the ***Paddock*** (enclosure where horses are ***exercised)***.

-*Jesus (Campos)* '***Grassy Field***'—'***JC***,' *which double as the initials of Jesus* C*hrist*—*also became a* **'*savior*'** *by distracting the shooter.* As a result of this 'heroic' act, he was invited to do an interview with reporters. But *Jesus* reportedly 'bolted' just before the cameras began to roll. **Jesus** (Campos) then disappeared for **3 days** (**Mathew 12:40**), finally being '**resurrected**' for his first and final interview on the Ellen show.

On the Ellen show, Campos appeared somewhat despondent as Ellen led him through a rudimentary explanation of the events of the night of the shooting, which was absent of *any* open-ended questions. She even showed a fancy diagram of the scene while *she* lead him through the running narrative, rather than the other way around.

At the end of the 'interview,' 'Shutterfly' awarded, *Jesus,* with a giant check for $25,000 dollars (a*hem*...'forbidden fruit?'). Ellen closes this interview by remarking to Jesus :

> 'I know you've had so many people asking for you to tell the story and talk about it and I understand your reluctance. **You're talking about it now and you're not going to talk about it again**. I don't blame you. Why relive it over and over?'

I will leave you with this parting thought concerning Ellen's complicity in all of this.... **Mandalay Bay is owned by MGM,** *who also owns the Ellen show!*

If you want to creep yourself out, watch the video and read the lyrics to the *Jason Aldean* song which signaled the bedlam, titled, **'They Don't Know.'** It is impossible to explain the creepiness factor of the video. I had intended to break it all down but there was no way to put all of the symbology into words without changing the direction of this entire paper.

One thing I *will* tell you, though, is that **the video setting is in a Grassy Field** in which a whole crowd of people stare at the camera despairingly, while flashing back and forth to a scene in which a Field is being **Harvested** by a combine! Let us not forget that the event itself was called '*Route **91 Harvest** Festival*,'

When considering the symbolism of a combine '**harvesting**' a '**grassy field**,' I would like for you to remember YHWH's symbolism of the *'chaff,'* the *'wheat and the tares,'* and the *'threshing floor.'* I would also like to point out the fact that, in the past, human sacrifice around the world, throughout time, has been associated with 'fertility' and bringing forth 'rain' from the gods in order to grow 'crops.' Aldean's music video for 'They Don't Know' incorporates *all of these elements; Apollo—the destroyer of **9:11**—is **known** as the* '**god of crops**.' What's more, even Aldean's *tour* was called *'They Don't Know!'* The ACM then awarded Jason Aldean with the honors of being 'Entertainer of the Year'....*Forbidden Fruit, anyone?*

If you want to *really* creep yourself out, watch the unedited version of the news interview showing Paddock's brother rambling for thirty minutes to reporters, while appearing to be terribly high on some stimulant. The gunman's brother drivels on, explaining how Paddock was a 'high roller' at the casinos and how much money he makes, and how he 'eats $10,000 dollar sushi lunches,' complimentary. (If you watch this crazy video, your questions pertaining to this heinous event will completely lay to rest.)

It appears as though the lost bough from the Garden of Eden is *still* sagging with fruit. This 'Forbidden Fruit' is extremely tempting if you don't have Christ in your life. You don't even need to look for it anymore since the 'Tree of the Knowledge of Good and Evil' has even been planted right in your child's school—in recent news a school in Florida made a big legal splash for allowing a group of satanists to circulate a coloring book titled 'After School Satan' in a *public* school.

There is a cartoon on adult swim in which a wild-eyed dog who is possessed by the devil, runs wild, decapitating people and having sex with the severed heads. The filth is called 'Mr. Pickles.' When I was a kid, my parents told me that the 'Smurfs' were demonic and even though I didn't see it then, *they were right*. What I am trying to demonstrate here is the evolution of evil in society, which gradually grows into the system of antichrist, where horrific events will occur more openly and even become acceptable practice.

During the 'witch burnings' of Europe, it was documented that peoples' own relatives even began to look-on romantically as their own family members were put to death. This evil *will* sneak up on us, too, *before we even know it*. I am *screaming* at the frogs in the pot because the water has now begun to release its first dances of steam but, *the frogs still seem very comfortable*.

30. Legs of Iron

There is so much shade cast upon the events of 9/11 that it would be impossible to summarize all of the nuances of the suspected players so, I will simply offer you the verses from Genesis 11 which will be followed up by a list of bullet points to prevent the confusion surrounding this horrible event from overtaking the beautiful message of this work. Genesis **11** :

> King James Version (KJV)
> **6** And the Lord said, Behold, **the people is one**, and **they have all one language**; and this they begin to do: and **now nothing will be restrained from them, which they have imagined to do.**
> **7** Go to, [1] **let us go down, and there confound their language**, that they may not understand one another's speech.
> **8** So [2] **the Lord scattered them abroad from thence upon the face of all the earth**: [3] **and they left off to build the city.**

- [1] **let us go down, and there confound their language,...** — We have seen more modern evolutions of this same technology when we saw the Spanish change the language of the entirety of the Americas from the evolved 'Native' American dialects to Spanish in Mexico, English in America, and French in Canada. William the Conquerer, who couldn't read or write, contributed more to the English language than any other single person. And his bloodline had no trouble creating new languages for the many countries which they conquered. These are all late examples of the same technology being described above in verse 7.

- [2] These slaves were '**scattered abroad upon the face of *all* the earth.**' This line illustrates that Nimrod did indeed use his Great Grandfather's boat technology to scatter these slaves around the world to build King Nimrod's cities '**abroad!**'
- [3] Then, '**they left off to build the city.**' This line tells you that the 'Mystery Babylon' of Revelation is really no 'mystery' at all since the word 'city' here is *singular. We* are all now living in the 'Mystery Babylon' discussed in Revelation.

The points below show the great symbolic parallels between The Tower of Babel and the destruction of the Twin Towers in NYC, as well as exposing the many satanic elements which still hover in the air which used to surround these Towers.

- On September 9/**11**, the Twin Towers were knocked down.
- The Tower of Babel account is found in Genesis **11.**
- Babel was the tallest building in the world when it was constructed and so were the Twin Towers when they were built.
- The two separate towers themselves formed the number **11**, which also symbolized the pillars of freemasonry; after the towers were knocked down, they formed a **1**.
- Revelation *9:11*—And they had a king over them, which is the **angel of the bottomless pit**, whose name in the Hebrew tongue is Abaddon, but

in the Greek tongue hath his name Apollyon. Remember, **Apollyon means** 'The Destroyer.'

- The two fountains at the foot of the new One World Trade Center make up the nation's largest manmade waterfalls; the fountains are officially called *Reflecting Absence*. If you look at the first words in bold in the last bullet point, you will notice that the *Reflecting Absence* fountains represent the 'bottomless pit' in Revelation 9:11. Adding to the grimy symbolism here, the fountains are black and have an infinity design which gives the appearance that the pools are in fact, 'bottomless.'
- A third building commonly referred to simply as 'building 7' fell and it wasn't even impacted by a plane; **the building's real name is *Salomon Brothers*—**King ***Solomon* is worshipped by the freemasons.** The companies occupying this building were involved in far too many scandals to list here.
- The architectural firm which 'won' the 'design contest' for replacing the Twin Towers was a single tower design, *just like the Tower of Babel.*
- The single tower design of **One World** Trade Center became the new tallest tower in the western hemisphere.
- The 'lucky architect' who drafted the 'winning design' was *David Childs*, whose firm is Skidmore, Owings & Merrill (SOM). Childs shares his alma mater, **Yale** *University*, with George Bush; Yale is home to The Order of Skull and Bones.
- 'Skull and Bones' rituals include grave robbery and using these bones to communicate with 'the gods.'
- One of the gods with whom Skull and Bones communicates, is **Baal**—The Twelve Hebrew Tribes of The Old Testament completely extinguished society after society of 'giants' and 'Canaanite' evildoers for

worshipping and sacrificing their babies to the same 'god' that The Order of Skull and Bones are still worshipping today: **Baal**.
- The 9/11 memorial museum, which is located in the basement of one of the old Towers, contains a giant 'memorial wall' in which many of the scattered human remains were placed; this is an ancient Greek witchcraft ritual. In ancient Greece and Rome, virgins—*or* otherwise—were sacrificed on the dirt of a building site, after which the body was buried under the site, as a sacrifice to 'the gods.' The museum *cave* features crumpled firetrucks, burnt airplane parts, timepieces and other personal items worn by victims, and all manner of the destroyer of 9/11's handiwork; it even features an obelisk made from an old steel beam, which was cleverly placed right next to the supposed 'memory wall.'
- The Memory Wall, containing these 'human remains,' is blue and seems to be a sort of revival of the Ishtar Gate of Babylon.
- David Childs, who designed One World Trade Center, was the personal architect for Osama bin Laden's father.
- Bin Laden's father is a billionaire who himself is an international tower builder and has done business with the Bushes for years.
- *Mohammed bin Awad bin Laden's* oldest son Salem was one of George Bush's first business partners. So, to clear the air here: Osama Bin Laden 'knocked the Towers down' and then we hired his father's architect to profit from cleaning up the mess—*this is controlled conflict 101.*
- Childs and bin Laden's father also collaborated to raise the **Burj Khalifa** which currently *is* the tallest tower in the world; its name translates to 'successor tower'—'**Antichrist Tower.**' *Burj* means 'Tower' and *Khalifa* means 'successor,' which is an Arabic word that is used interchangeably

with the word 'antichrist'—the *successor* to Nimrod, the first tower builder.
- The company who won the *construction project* for the new *One World Trade Center* was *Tishman Construction* who also famously constructed and resided in the infamous **666** 5th Avenue building.
- The *Kushners*, the family of Trump's son in law, Jared *Kushner*, bought the sinister **666** 5th Avenue in 2007 for a record breaking 1.8 Billion dollars.
- **666** Fifth Avenue is now connected to Rockefeller Center by a breezeway—*Rockefeller* is a well-known Skull and Bones family. There is a gold statue of Prometheus—*the Greek version of King Nimrod*—as Rockefeller Center's centerpiece.
- The company *Lucent Technologies*, which has designed and is experimenting with the 'RFID chip' *for tracking humans,* also resides in **666** 5th Avenue.
- Donald Trump was billing Jared Kushner as the man who would 'bring peace to the Middle East,' long before he was even elected. Daniel 9:27: 'And **he shall confirm the covenant with many for one week** [7 years]: and in the midst of the week [3.5 years] he shall cause the sacrifice and the oblation to cease, and for the overspreading of abominations he shall make it desolate, even until the consummation, and that determined shall be poured upon the desolate.' This could just be a very unlikely coincidence but, if this is not the final account spoken-of in Daniel, it sure seems that this presidency is desperately attempting to fit the prophecies.
- Despite the trust placed in Kushner, for making peace in the Middle East, Kushner has no diplomatic experience whatsoever.

- Ivanka Trump converted to Judaism in order to marry into the Kushner family.
- '**Kush**' was the name of one of Noah's sons.
- Jared **Kush**ner's father Charles Kushner is also a Tower developer. **Charles was convicted of illegal campaign contributions, tax evasion, and witness tampering**. Charles Kushner served time in federal prison and resumed playing monopoly with his *Tower* development company, upon his release.
- From the side angle, One World Trade Center appears to be a giant, gold pyramid.

I could literally do this for days but you get the picture.

Reuniting King Nimrod's Scattered Citizens

When you boil it all down, this is what happened: According to The Bible, after The Flood, King Nimrod built the first 'Tower,' which was really a *pyramid*. He then used Grandpa Noah's boat technology to 'scatter' Noah's own offspring for seeding new cities allover the world, 'confounding their languages' to make it easier to manipulate them independently in every way.

The Bible accurately predicts that this sphere of despotism would eventually reunite, which is an event that the sons of darkness have been desperately attempting to finalize since God destroyed their first abominable World Empire in The Great Flood.

Rather than the original WTC project combining all of their resources to make a super-high Tower, the *Twin Towers* were built in our times to represent the two legs of the fused Roman Empire, which had been manipulating the 12 tribes independently for ages. Along comes Bin Laden—*a Bush family business partner*—to knock down the 'Twin Towers.' American airlines **Flight 11** struck the first Tower. A **United** plane struck the second tower, '**uniting**' the '*Twin* **Towers**' into *'One World'* Trade Center. This satanic, mass human sacrifice ritual signaled the rise of the **one world** leader, *Apollyon of Revelation 9/11*.

Only a couple of years before the Twin Towers were **united**, a large group of Airlines from allover the world formed a giant affiliate network called **OneWorld**. This means that the fuselage of American Airlines Flight **11** would've had a *OneWorld* decal freshly adhered next to the door when it kicked off the event which signaled this epic moment for the sons of darkness—*the moment when the Twelve Tribes re*-unite.

You may have already noticed one of these *OneWorld* decals next to the door when you boarded *your* last flight; now you know why it's there. And, yet somehow no one has even raised an eyebrow to the fact that the heartwarming new name for the WTC *was identical to that of an advertising gimmick for the Airline that had hit the building.*

> Note: The two Towers combining as 'One' is also how the Country music festival in Vegas—*91* Harvest—earned its name; *after* the synthesis of 9—*11*, the two towers combined forming a '*1*.' This new synthesis turned 9*11* into simply, 9…*1*, or *91* Harvest. I am

sure that from now on we can expect some ugly things on September 1.

A Yale graduate designed, *Burj Khalifa*, which means 'Antichrist Tower.' *Antichrist Tower* now replaces Babel as the tallest tower in the world and **it was built by Bin Laden's dad**. Mohamed Bin Laden's architect designed One World Trade Center to look like a giant pyramid and incorporated a 'memory wall' within which contains the human remains of *many* 9/11 victims, *underneath* the 'pyramid' ; this is ritual magic which dates back to Greek times. On the 'memory wall' is a quote :

> 'No day shall erase you from the memory of time'

There is much controversy surrounding this 'misplaced quote' since, Virgil's *The Aeneid was a story telling of the founding of Rome*. Even Caroline Alexander, a reporter at the New York Times was finding this disturbing as she penned her article titled, **Out of Context**. Here is a small excerpt from her concerning piece :

> 'Some families of the victims have criticized the planned memorial because they are offended by the prospect of sharing the resting place of their loved ones with museum-going strangers. Because the structure will be built seven stories below the spot where the twin towers once stood, visitors will have to venture underground to pay their respects, a prospect that also is not comforting.'

Caroline Alexander goes on to explain *how* this Virgil quote is Taken out of Context, remarking the following :

> 'Virgil's epic relates the trials of the unhappy Trojan hero Aeneas, who, as Troy burns, flees with the remnants of his family and people to his ships and the sea, eventually winding up in Italy, where it is his destiny to lay the foundation of what will become Rome.'

This poem was written to tell the story of the rising of the Roman Empire! Using this poem on this 'memory wall' literally symbolizes the beginning of a 'revived' Roman empire spoken-of by the Prophet Daniel when he advised King Nebuchadnezzar about the 'statue' he saw in his dream; the Twin Towers certainly seem to be the '**legs of iron**' spoken-of by Daniel, *which were knocked down by an object coming from the sky!* These 'legs of iron' are symbolic on several levels but, as always the layers of symbolism in The Bible are so thick that it indeed becomes The Living Word. Daniel 2 :

> King James Version (KJV)
> **33** His legs of iron, [1] **his feet part of iron and part of clay**.
> **34** Thou sawest till that [2] **a stone was cut out without hands**, which smote the image upon his feet were of iron and clay, and brake them to pieces.

- [1] '... **his feet part of iron and part of clay**.'—The Towers were made **of iron** and their '**feet**' are called '**footers**!' Concrete would have been poured into the forms of the *footers*, around the steel rebar, literally mixing '***iron and clay!***' The exact terminology used in the KJV is '**miry clay**' ; according to google, here is the definition of 'miry' : very muddy [soupy muddy] or boggy. If you have ever watched concrete being poured this word describes the pouring of the 'feet' of the Twin Towers perfectly.

- [2] '**a stone was cut out without hands…**' — This 'stone without hands' comment certainly sounds like an airplane to me. That this 'stone' was '***cut*** without hands,' shows that it was a symmetrical and polished type of shape, **with arms**. If it were just any raw rock or 'millstone,' Daniel would have simply called the object a 'stone.' If you were living in ancient times and were trying to describe in the words of the day what happened after having witnessed the events of 9/11, *this would sure sum up it up in a sentence*. Once, again, I give you Daniel 2 :

King James Version (KJV)
34 Thou sawest till that **a stone was cut out without hands, which smote the image upon his feet that were of iron and clay, and brake them to pieces.**

A jet airplane could be the *only* logical explanation for what is described in the passage above. Below we will finish our study of Daniel 2; the scripture below describes exactly what happened on 9/11 after the towers fell. Daniel 2 :

King James Version (KJV)
35 Then was the iron, the clay, the brass, the silver, and the gold, **[1] broken to pieces together, and became like the chaff of the**

summer threshing floors; and the wind carried them away, that no place was found for them: [2] **and the stone that smote the image became a great mountain, and filled the whole earth**.

[1] '...**broken to pieces together, and became like the chaff of the summer threshing floors**...' For Daniel, who was witnessing this event as a spectator from the past, the above description would've been *very* accurate. Daniel would have seen the towers: '**break to pieces**,' '**and the wind carried them away...**' ; since, the towers were virtually hollow compared to the pyramids of Daniel's day and, after falling, a giant cloud of smoke and flying debris floated through Manhattan, *for miles*, giving the appearance that the towers themselves 'were carried away.'

[2] '**and the stone that smote the image became a great mountain, and filled the whole earth**.' If you google image 'ground zero 9/11'—or, *if you witnessed it on the news a million times like I did*—the image of the '**great mountain**' of debris is now burned in your mind and matches sentence **2** perfectly.

> Note: In *Sacred Scroll of Seven Seals*, the prelude to this book, I discovered a perfect match for the same event within the sister prophecies in the Book of Revelation; the parallels are indescribable.

Just after this 'handless' object hits the empirical statue and crumbles the 'legs of iron,' a giant 'millstone' hits earth, and the New Jerusalem forms in which the men who are left on the 'threshing floor' will live; those who've done wrong to others are 'baled and burned.' This *could* signal that some crazy times are *afoot* for our generation. Daniel also predicted in this chapter that the 'Iron and clay' 'shall not cleave one to another,' which shows that whatever comes next *will not work*. Most Biblical scholars agree that this is symbolic of a modern restoration of the Roman Empire.

This adds a lot more suspicion to the Virgil quote above, especially since it's written upon a wall which contains human remains and, burying human remains underneath a structure was a dark ritual for lending good fortune to a new building in Greek and Roman days.

It is bone-chilling to now know that, *today*, Nimrod's ancient plans for expanding Babylon into a *World* Empire and then bringing us all back together '**as one**' world to again all speak '**one language**,' is coming to its final conclusion. Let us look at the corresponding passage once again, in Genesis 11 :

> King James Version (KJV)
> **6** And the Lord said, Behold, **the people is one**, and **they have all one language; and this** [building towers] **they begin to do**: and **now nothing will be restrained from them, which they have imagined to do**.

Technology is a wonderful thing but, it seems that from the beginning of recorded history man has had a terrible time not wielding their discoveries with the hand of evil. As hard as it is to accept that almost everything in our culture is a lie or an abomination, this *is* the system of antichrist. I don't like it either but the scriptures did *not* say that, 'some of the people would be deceived' ; the deception was *much* greater than that. Matthew 24 :

> King James Version (KJV)
> 24 For there shall arise false Christs, and false Prophets, and shall shew great signs and wonders; **insomuch that, if it were possible, they shall deceive the very elect**.

Donald means '**world ruler**' and himself is a '**tower**-builder' who lives at the top of Trump *'tower.'* *I hope I've grabbed your attention.* It seems that we may have a front row seat to the final Bible 'Story' which started out with 'In the beginning' so long ago. Face it. **We are, unsuspectingly, Biblical characters who are now watching the *'Revelation'* of *'Genesis 11'*** — *the finality of the Greatest Bible* account of all time. And if not soon, *we are hair-raisingly close which means that we are witnessing the forerunning prophecies as they unfold on screen, right in our own living rooms.*

31. Verginia, USA

Before we move forward in the text, I would like to remind you once more of the NYT reporter's remarks concerning the 'Out of Context' quote placed upon the 'memory wall' containing human remains beneath One World Trade Center :

> 'Virgil's epic relates the trials of the unhappy Trojan hero Aeneas, who, as Troy burns, flees with the remnants of his family and people to his ships at sea nearby, eventually landing in Italy, where it is his destiny to lay the foundation of what will become Rome.'

Virgil's story, *The Aeneid,* gives us a candid look inside the very collapse and rebirth of the system of antichrist. *Aeneas's* story is the very account of the elite bloodline calling upon the collapse of one antichrist society and the 'rise of the Phoenix' which is the transition into the rebirth of the benign beginnings of another antichrist society to begin the whole cycle again.

This 'story' clearly illustrates the elite bloodline saving themselves for the purpose of acting as 'the gods' of their fresh empire. You will now see that these events are planned-for and even harvested when the *fruit* of this 'system' becomes ripe.

Another similar work, *Titus Livius' History of Rome* is an *extensive* collection of writing which documents the *founding* of the *new* Roman empire. *'Livy's'* account picks up where *Virgil's* left off, the period from the arrival of *Aeneas* sometimes referred to as *Ab Urbe Condita*, to the City's founding in 753 BC.

So, *Livy's* account of the social implosion above tells of a **virgin** girl who Appius Claudius was very fond of to say the least. *Claudius* was a powerful member of the decemvirs, a committee of ten men chosen in the place of *'consuls'* to draw up the tables of Roman law. **Verginia's** father, *Lucius 'Verginius'—a respected centurion*—had already promised his daughter's hand to another fella. So when Lucius became aware of Claudius's intentions, he became very angry. Claudius then kidnapped the virgin on her way to school and acted as if she were his slave in order to 'legally' obtain her as his property.

The crowds in the Forum were becoming very hostile over the situation, which was greatly publicized; the citizens had already been terribly distraught over the decemvirs **for not calling the proper elections, taking bribes, and other abuses**. It seemed that their 'democratic' society were returning to the old Rule by *Kings*; this system had been overthrown just decades prior. (Those citizens too were under the impression that they were some sort of evolved democratic society.)

As the story goes—*the short version*—the citizens of their society were provoked into an uproar as these political 'abuses' began to fester. *(Isn't *this old story beginning to sound familiar?)* The case was brought before the decemvirs in a vibrating Forum, of which Claudius himself led; he would not even allow the girl's father to speak.

Claudius declared the girl to be *his* 'slave' and, having an armed guard with him, accused the citizens of sedition. The supporters left due to the threatening guard and Verginius begged to speak to his daughter which, *was allowed*. But when he approached the girl, however, he brandished a knife and stabbed the girl—the only way she could truly be 'free.' The events which followed triggered the entire collapse of Troy, spawning Aeneas's hasty getaway to Italy and thus the birth of Rome.

The running fairy tale concerning the origin of the state of Virginia's name is as follows, taken from the website of Virginia's library system :

> What is the meaning of the name Virginia? 'Virginia was named for Queen Elizabeth I of England, who was known as the Virgin Queen. Historians think the English adventurer Sir Walter Raleigh suggested the name about 1584. That year, Elizabeth gave Raleigh permission to colonize the Virginia region.'

You now know that Virginia was symbolic of a modern revolution of the old Roman Empire. If you've done any reading on this place, just as was the NYT reporter who questioned the Virgil quote at the 911 museum, *you should be concerned—**gravely concerned**!*

Remember, this whole Verginia debacle is the event which 'caused Troy to burn to the ground,' **leaving 'Aeneas to flee from the wreckage to form Rome**.' And, *Aeneas,* is the same fella who Virgil was writing about when he penned the quote which now emblazons the 'memory wall' containing those human remains, *7 stories beneath the WTC.*

The Virginia State flag now depicts a Roman Soldier standing next to a dead fellow with a crown sitting next to him; the quote beneath the fiasco reads, 'Death to Tyrants,' which doubles as the motto of the **Society of Jesus**—the **Jesuit**, priests' of the **Roman Catholic** Church, aka 'the pope's marines.' *Incredibly,* the *US* Marine Corps uses this similar slogan—'Sic Semper Fidelis'—in **Latin**.

And that, *my friend*, is how the State of *Virginia* really got her name.

32. Revolution 9:11

So Aeneas escaped the wreckage of Troy and founded Rome which *itself* was a revival of the same system of antichrist that had just leveled Troy. I know that we all stare at the leftover stones of emptiness littering these ancient sites and imagine that there is little to be learned about what had occurred there but, our ancient history was *all* carefully documented for the posterity of those in charge; *though it has mostly been reduced to 'myth' for we 'vulgar.'*

To avoid the intended historic confusion surrounding the infinite *Greco-Roman* writings, you and I will fast forward to the laying of the foundations for a temple in *Rome*, originally dedicated to the god **Saturn**—*the word from which the name '***satan***' was derived.* These 'temples' were a modern evolution of the previously discussed 'high places' explained in The Bible, *from one end to the other.* Most of the Old Testament is composed of accounts in which the Twelve Tribes cleansed the world of these same tribes of Canaanite, baby-killing giants.

The temple dedicated to satan which once stood atop ancient Rome's '**Capitol**ine **Hill**' has now been moved to America—Rome's *new* Capitol. And 'Statuary Hall' is replete with *our* new Roman 'gods.' This satanic temple has been rebuilt in *every* modern evolution of this same empire, which *must* stretch all the way back to ancient Babylon. And, as you will soon see, a literal form of the same devil worship is now taking place in a dark, clandestine 'grove' in America, today, by all of these new 'gods.'

The Capitol City of Rome is world famous for its proximity to a grouping of '**seven hills**,' which is how it came to be *known* as the **City of Seven Hills**. **Capitoline Hill** directly overlooked the 'Roman Forum'—the complex of government buildings which housed *Rome's* 'head' of state—the governors of *their* Roman society.

The cliff marking the edge of Capitoline Hill **was once named the Tarpeian Rock after the Vestal *Virgin* who was first tossed from this hill**. This fact points to even more disturbing evidence for *our* reverence of the name 'Virginia,' which doubles as the name of the state in which our new Rome was founded. The intentions of the founders of our new Rome become perfectly clear when we remember that the British royals, *who founded Virginia in the first place*, named *their* corporation, 'The *Virginia* Company.'

Countless prisoners—*and virgins*—in ancient Rome followed the Vestal Virgin to her horrible fate, since tossing people from *'the Hill'* became a common method of **capital** punishment. Veritably, this is also how the term **capital** *punishment* came into existence.

The word 'Capitol,' itself, earned its name after the head of a man was found when constructing the second temple on Capitoline Hill. (Remember, this was an age-old ritual of human sacrifice **which has been recy-**

cled at the 9/11 '**museum**.') Ancient sources refer to the name of this hill as '**kaput**' which means 'head'— *'decapitation'* is a latin based word which we still use in nearly identical form. Now the '**head**' of every state and country is referred to as its '**Capitol**.' As a matter of fact, during excavation, the old temple was found to house an entire cemetery buried beneath it, *just as we planted a mausoleum beneath One World Trade Center.* Remarkably we find the same 'head' symbolism at the grounds of Christ's Crucifixion in Jerusalem, since, calvary too means 'dead head' or 'skull' ; we now use a version of this word to refer to factions of our military when we refer to them as: cavalry. Moreover, the word 'cranium' evolved from the greek word from which the word calvary was derived: 'Kranion.' Is this simply more elusion to the ancient order of Skull and Bones?

The temple upon *our* Capitol Hill now cleverly *doubles* as our head of state, which is great camouflage for a 'government building' which is really an evolution of a Roman temple dedicated to satan.

Washington DC—Rome's New Capitol
The statue on top of the pantheon that today we call the 'Capitol Dome' is Athena. *Athena* is a Greek goddess and she is the daughter of Zeus—*yet another name for satan!* The City of *Athens* was even named for Athena who doubled as the City's god, *just as she doubles as ours*. Minus the dome, the architecture of *our* Capitol Building is nearly identical to the that of the Parthenon—*the temple dedicated to Athena in ancient Greece.* What's more, the Vatican shares the same sacred geometrical lines as these two temples. And all of the aforementioned structures, which are

near-duplicates to the ancient 'Temple of Saturn,' featured Jacob's Pillars which elevate a pyramid—*a triangle*—*unto the heavens*.

Athena, went on to be a member of the ancient Roman 'Council of Nine' which Anton Lavey—*founder of the satanic church*—claimed to have '*re*-established' in 1966. Lavey coined the year 1966 '*anno satanas'—year one of the rule of satan (though, I believe this to be another one of his lies, and that his reign is coming to its final conclusion)*. The two quotes below were taken out of the prologue of Lavey's *satanic 'bible.'* They give us clear insight, from the dark side, as to the final mechanism which will produce Apollo's very last terrible appearance to the human race. Remember: *this was the same 'destroyer' spoken-of by John of Patmos, in his Book of Revelation!*

'The gods of the right-hand path have bickered and quarreled for an entire age of earth. Each of these deities and their respective priests and ministers have attempted to find wisdom in their own lies. The ice age of religious thought can last but a limited time in this great scheme of human existence. The gods of wisdom-defiled have had their saga, and their millennium [speaking of the 'Millennial Reign of Christ] hath become as reality. Each, with his own "divine" path to paradise, hath accused the other of heresies and spiritual indiscretions…'

'…The twilight is done. A glow of new light is borne out of the night and Lucifer is risen, once more to proclaim: "This is the age of Satan! Satan Rules the Earth!" The gods of the unjust are dead. This is the morning of magic, and undefiled wisdom. The FLESH prevaileth and a great Church shall be builded, consecrated in its name. No longer shall man's salvation be dependent on his self-denial. And it will be known that the world of the flesh and the living shall be the greatest preparation for any and all eternal delights! REGIE SATANAS! AVE SATANAS! HAIL SATAN!'

It's the **Revolution** '**Number 9**' whom the Beatles driveled-on about in 1968—spoken-of in ***Revelation 9*** in The Bible—the rise of 'the destroyer' who had previously destroyed Troy. This is the spirit of Nimrod—the first great city builder. Today we stand at the end of an unbroken string of burnt cities which, no doubt, lead all the way back to ancient Babylon. And, it seems, the human race is poised to witness *the destroyer's* final performance: the *destruction* of a civilization which now includes all of mankind.

The paragraph below describes this *council of nine,* who Anton Lavey claimed to have re-established in 1966 :

In order to *punish* man, Zeus and eight more of 'the gods' united forming *the Council of Nine*. The council members were **Athena**, **Apollo** (Abaddon—'the destroyer' of Revelation 9:11), Aphrodite, Demeter, Hephaestus, Hera, Hermes, Poseidon and **Zeus**.

The Prophecies of the Cumaean Sibyl
Here's where the 'Michelangelo Code' comes *back* into play in order to help us solve this great mystery…Do you remember Michelangelo's paint-

ing of the six fingered 'Lady-Giant' on the ceiling of the Sistine Chapel? Remarkably, this prophetess—*who was discussed at the opening of this adventure*—now rejoins us in our story. The *Cumaean Sibyl* was a demon possessed fortune teller whose work was so accurate that she was revered by these ancients to the point of herself being made a god. The story of Aeneas, the Sibyl, Athena, and *the Destroyer*, goes something like this:

Aeneas made a stop at **Cumae**, on the coast of Campania in southern Italy. While there, Aeneas visited the temple of Apollo where the Sibyl was the priestess who presided over the Apollonian oracle at Cumae, a Greek colony located near Naples, Italy. The Sibyl's prophetic inspiration was received within a deeply recessed cave on the flank of a *hill*, where she heard hundreds of voices which, *she claimed* would become 'oracular answers.' You can still visit this cave which still exists nearly as it did in the days of Aeneas, *as long as you and the family arrive between 9 and 6:00 pm; tours of the grotto are scheduled on every day of the week.*

It was deep within this cave in the side of a mountain that Aeneas expressed his desires to Apollo, in which he asked for the kingdom which he'd been promised. In exchange for dominion over the entire world—*king Nimrod's old title*—Aeneas promised *the destroyer* of Revelation 9/11 that he **would build a stunning temple of marble to Apollo *and* also one for his sister, Athena.**

(Aeneas also promised that he would appoint festive days in Apollo's honor and to obey his orders till the end of time. September Eleven seems to be just that. 'Independence Day,' too, is an ancient holiday on which to make bloody sacrifices in the honor of Zeus, and to celebrate those who were 'sacrificed' on the battlefield.)

The Sibyl's hair flailed about and her breast pulsed with great tremors as she foamed at the mouth. Her body convulsed and vibrated until she submitted to the power of *the destroyer;* her eyes then rolled to the top of her head as her body went limp, when the gates to hades swung wide open and she delivered the oracle. This scene is identical to the description of Bill and Hillary's visit to Haiti described in Clinton's memoir's, titled, 'My Life' : Perhaps this is the exact point in time at which these two also became possessed by the demons who our leaders are required to invite into their vessels, just as king Saul—the very first king of Judah—had done.

After thousands of years of *horrible* world wars, it looks like Aeneas fulfilled *his* end of the bargain and built *Athena* her new 'temple' in Washington DC. And now, it appears, Apollo was issued *his* in New York City. The temple to Apollo which replaced the Twin Towers has a Carrara marble subway corridor like nothing you've ever seen, and the temple dedicated to Athena on Capitol Hill has an eighteen foot statue of Athena on its spire.

Take a stroll around DC, *after finishing this book*, then stop and look up at Athena's statue, which proudly stands atop the Capitol Dome in DC, and every hair on your back will likely stand erect. It appears that Aeneas finally declared this new world empire when Bush stuck that, 'Out of Context'

Virgil quote on the side of the *Ishtar-gate-blue wall*, deep within the bowels of '**One World**' trade center. Having seen this Apollonian complex with my own eyes, I gotta say that Aeneas gave *the destroyer* more than he'd bargained for.

According to *multiple* ancient legends, Nimrod's [Osiris's] 'severed penis' would need to be located before his physical 'return to earth.' The erection of **One World** Trade Center—also a giant obelisk—represents this long-awaited discovery of Nimrod's lost penis. As if all of this *weren't* bone chilling enough, the original manuscripts of the Cumaean Sibyl's prophecies— *outlining the final apocalypse via the return of 'the destroyer'*—were kept on **Capitol**ine Hill *within* the 'Temple of Satan.' Below, is the incredible account of the return of 'Apollo' *in the prophetic book of Revelation 9/11* :

> King James Version (KJV)
> And they had a king over them, which is the angel of the bottomless pit, whose name in the Hebrew tongue is Abaddon, but in the Greek tongue hath his name **Apollyon [Apollo]**.

Michelangelo actually painted 5 sibyls on the ceiling of the Sistine Chapel, who were each placed near an image of *Apollo—the destroyer. This imagery fits the ongoing narrative*, since each of these Sibyls *presided* over a temple of Apollo in ancient times, *and* each was in communication with *the destroyer, just as was the Cumaean Sibyl*. Michelangelo painted these images *on the ceiling in yellow and gold* because Apollo was a 'sun god' just like every other head deity (which explains Revelation 12:1), in nearly every empire, within every culture, around the world.

This proves that the Vatican *was never* dedicated to Christ, but, instead—*just like One World Trade Center*—it was another promised *temple to Apollo* with a cemetery beneath it. Whether it was Ra in Egypt, Baal for the Canaanites—*the hundreds of other 'sun gods' in every culture around the world*—or the pope and presidents today, it's all just sun god worship: the worship of king Nimrod. Even when our American presidents 'lie in state,' they do so under the Capitol dome which is painted similarly to Michelangelo's work in the Sistine Chapel.

The fresco on the Capitol Dome, painted by **Greek-Italian** artist **Constantino Brumidi** in 1865, even includes an image of Washington sitting between Apollo and Athena, after being beamed up to heaven. Brumidi's fresco includes many other evolutions of King Nimrod, including: 'Mercury,' and 'Neptune.' The name of the heavenly painting on the ceiling of the *new* Capitoline Hill is, *The Apotheosis of Washington*. Apotheosis means: *the elevation of someone to divine status—deification—'becoming god.'* Which means that, when American presidents die, we honor *them* with an identical deification ritual as every other evolution of this same empire, from Babylon to Egypt to Rome, have practiced.

The head 'god' of Hinduism, who, in their tongue goes by the name, *Shiva*, shares the same name and agenda as Apollo: *destruction. What is more*, if you will recall, *Shiva* is the same 'god' to which Alexander the Great's monk, *Calanus*, was sacrificed **by engulfing himself in flames**, after uttering the word's: '*We shall meet in Babylon.*' This immediately calls into question CERN's, giant, electronic, magic circle, with which scientists have been hunting for the supposed, 'dark' matter, and a, so-called, 'god particle.' Why? *You ask*....The headquarters of the CERN project on 'North Star Avenue'—in the *United Kingdom*—has a large statue of the *Indian* destroyer, *Shiva*, on her front lawn, by which videos of strange magic rituals and mock human sacrifice have been filmed.

The French town in which CERN is situated is called *Saint-Genus-Poilly*. The name *Pouilly* is taken from the Latin name 'Appolliacum' which means: *Apollo*. And the Latin *suffix,* 'iacum,' denotes possession. This means that the name of the City in which Cern is located translates to: 'this land belongs to Apollo.' The spot hosted a temple of Apollo in ancient times and the people who lived there believed the spot to be a 'gateway to the underworld.'

Being the location of an ancient 'temple dedicated to Apollo,' it is important to note that—just like the ancient, oracular, complexes were all built around a cave—the collider too is located at a depth ranging from 164 to 574 feet underground; this new *temple of Apollo*, is contained in a **circular** tunnel, with a circumference of 16.6 miles. So, to recap, Cern is located on the grounds of an, ancient Greek, oracular, *Apollonion complex,* and its modern-day, electronic temple of Apollo, has a statue of Shiva—*standing inside a circle*—placed on her lawn in front of the new temple. *And*, Shiva too means, 'the destroyer,' which doubles as the meaning of the name of 'Apollo,' the beast of Revelation 9/11.

That Alex was in collusion with this high-level, Hindu, magician of *destruction*, shows an ancient connection between the extermination of societies *and India;* this also fills in the blanks for East *India* Company's unhealthy love affair with the South East Asian country, which came at the cost of the *destruction* of well-over a hundred million Indian lives under British rule. The monks of 'Tyre' who recorded the Russells' exploits in the 'little book,' which sparked the discovery that kicked off this entire book series, *were also Hindi* (Tyre being the same city which Nebuchadnezzar and Alex the great, both, flattened! And, as outlined, these were events which were both predicted in multiple Biblical accounts!).

We *know* that Alexander the Great's empire was worshipping *the destroyer* of Revelation **9:11**—*'Apollo'*—when his troops 'struck fear in the hearts of men,' women, and children, during *his* conquest of the known world. As a youth, Alexander *modeled* as Apollo the destroyer. His likeness was then engraved on statues and coins issued by his father, *Philip II of Macedon, who cheerfully foretold Alexander the Great's rise to 'greatness,' long before these events had even occurred!* In the wake of the destruction caused by Alexander the Great, temples of Apollo were spread across his new empire; these shiny temples were simply a continuation of the fulfillment of Aeneas's promises to the Cumaean Sibyl to: 'build temples to Apollo,' and 'worship him forever.' And just think: a quote from Aeneas's adventure, *the Aeneid*, now romantically adorns the outer wall of the necropolis deep within the cave beneath George Bush's *newest* temple of Apollo.

Alexander the Great was simply a dupe savior who was born and programmed to bring about a scheduled, empirical, changing of the guard—*an event which had also been predicted by Daniel centuries prior.* All of the evidence points to these ancient Babylonian/*Hindu* monks having overseen Alex's entire march of *destruction*, which also brings into question Hitler and *his* crew's unhealthy fascination with India. The mountain of evidence for this is worthy of its own publication but just to point out a couple of Indian fingerprints which were found at the scene of Hitler's crimes: a) Hitler's lead henchman, *Heinrich Himmler*, wouldn't even leave home without having a copy of the *Bhagavad Gita* in his pocket. And: b) The swastika has been used by hundreds of cultures including the *American* '**Indians**,' but, in ancient, **India**, the swastika has remained prevalent from the times of Babylon right up until today!

In India, the swastika is even used *side-by-side* with the so-called, 'Jewish,' Babylonian 'star of David.' During the times of the Old Testament, the swastika was chiseled into the rock adorning temples of baal—another place where humans were ritually thrown into a furnace. Looking back, it all seems so obvious. But those in the past would've been technologically-insulated from the information with which we have easily tracked these demons all the way back to India, today; this is why the internet will force the final evolution of a scam which has worked over-and-over-again; it is a wheel which they mistakenly think will turn forever.

The yellow *star of 'David'* has been resurrected many times by the Catholic Church, *throughout history*, in their countless successful attempts to, mark, segregate, oppress, round-up, and slaughter all of we 'jews' ; this endlessly recycled technology is the single-greatest factor for *our* dead-ended bloodline-connections to the 'Lost' Tribes. The Vatican's ugly actions caused the 'jewish' heritage *of all races* to become a stain on the pages of a family's genealogy, in order to prevent this amazing, cabalistic, technology for the organization of men, from resurfacing and challenging *their* authority; however, the six-pointed star on the pope's miter dangles *their* secret 'Jewish' lineage in all of our faces. When it comes down to it, most families have connections to Judaism which they don't openly profess. As a result, this bit of technology has, mistakenly, pigeonholed Judaism as a race instead of its true meaning: Judaism is a religion! Not a race! We are all connected by blood to these multicolored, 'Jewish' Tribes!

Now we have a solid connection between, India and the top brass in Nazi Germany who were also nosing around the remains of ancient Babylon before *and after* Hitler attempted to take over the world, Alexander the Great who *died* in Babylon and *did* take control of the entire world, the Vatican, and the founders of Washington DC who programmed the Greek version of this ancient Babylonian destroyer into all of *our* architecture, political mechanics, and 'educational' programs; after which, we *also* took control over the entire world. Since even the port city which was commandeered for the founding of Washington DC—**Alexandria**, Virginia—was *named* for **Alexander** the Great, perhaps we should take this type of destructive 'predictive programming' quite seriously.

In Babylonian, Indian, Egyptian, Persian, Greek, Roman—and now the American—cultures, *the destroyer* has had his way with our precious people. In more recent times, Apollo *the destroyer* follows the more-benign Athena into a nation's culture, and leads these empires into the same cycle of 'destruction' which the Hindu's claim to be the very 'genesis of creation' itself; just like every other empire, we are deceived and, by the same social programming, we too are preparing for the final march to our deaths.

The erection of One World Trade Center signals this great birth of Apollo, *the destroyer of 9/11—Nimrod—*into our culture; this event was known as 'the rise of the Phoenix' to cultures spanning the folds of time. This is precisely how the region in which the City of Tyre resided became known as: ancient 'Phoenicia' : The City of Tyre was burnt to the ground by both *Nebuchadnezzar* and *Alexander the Great, as predicted by Jeremiah, Amos and Ezekiel, and then rebuilt twice!* If you read the legend of the Phoenix, you will likely shutter. The Sibyl's prophecies were, no doubt, the same ancient instructions for raising and burning cities.

This explains the strange pose in which our 'American' eagle is placed on US seals, along with every other nations' symbolic birds: They all represent this 'prophetic' 'rising of the Phoenix'—*Prometheus, the Eagle, and the liver.* (The fact that the legendary Phoenix actually boldly served as the original *Emblem of the United States* confirms this notion.) By naming the *Missions* which landed man on the moon 'Apollo,' we are paying homage to the same ancient, satanic, anti-Christian deity; it appears that Nimrod's *metaphorical* tower of Babel (technology) has now, truly, reached unto the heavens. Genesis 11:

> [4] And they said, Go to, let us build us a city and a tower, ***whose top may reach *unto heaven*;** and let us make us a name, lest we be scattered abroad upon the face of the whole earth. NASA's use of the name of Saturn for the name of an ICBM (an **I**nter**C**ontinental

Ballistic **m**issile, which delivered nuclear ***destruction***) denotes our deep esoteric attachment to these early evolutions of the sun 'god' satan. The Lunar Module **Eagle** was then attached to these nuclear delivery systems, in place of a warhead, and slingshotted to the moon.

* Note: A clue in the symbolic Book of Revelation, in Chapter 18, points back to the above account of the Tower of Babel when John writes:

> '4 And I heard another voice from heaven, saying, Come out of her, my people, that ye be not partakers of her sins, and that ye receive not of her plagues.'
> 5 For ****her sins have reached unto heaven***, and God hath **remembered** her iniquities.

This profound eagle symbolism which represents the arrival of the antichrist—and which, *did* in fact 'reach unto heaven—becomes terribly frightening when we listen to old recordings of Neil Armstrong famously uttering the words, 'the Eagle has landed.' Let us not forget that this phrase was followed up with Armstrong saying: 'That's one small step for man, one **giant** leap for mankind.' Perhaps this moment was another symbolic statement which officially announced the return of Apollo, 'the destroyer' of Revelation 9/11.

The lady-giant *Sibyl's* prophecies concerning this return of *the destroyer* were carefully kept in a work known as the *Sibylline Books* (Latin: Libri

Sibyllini). According to tradition, **the books were purchased from the Sibyl by the *final king of Rome*, after which they were used by 'the senate' on Capitoline Hill in 'times of trouble.**' This tells us that, without a doubt, the brilliant instructions for Rome's new 'Christian' empire, and their invention of our fake two-party-democracy/shadow government, were all written into the Sibyl's apocalyptic plan—*a plan which John's Book of Revelation is screaming at us from the past!*

Once again, below is the quote taken from Virgil's work, *The Aeneid,* which has been regurgitated upon the necropolis wall deep within the cave beneath the new temple of *Apollo, One World Trade Center*—a contemporary revival of the entire *Apollonian* oracular complex of *Cumae* :

'No day shall erase you from the memory of time'

Astonishingly, another familiar Virgil quote resides above the pyramid on the one dollar bill; it reads *'novus ordo seclorum,'* also in Latin. Many conspiracy buffs claim that this Virgil phrase constitutes the first known use of the phrase: *'New World Order.'* And though this notion is wrongfully criticized by the established order, what we *know* to be true about this Virgil-phrase is perhaps far more disturbing. The phrase is a reference to the fourth *Eclogue* of Virgil, which contains the passage below in lines 5-8; I certainly hope that you are sitting down for this one:

5—'Ultima Cumaei venit iam carminis aetas;'
'Now comes the final era of the Sibyl's song;'

6—'Magnus ab integro **saeclorum nascitur ordo.**'
'**The great order of the ages is born anew.**'

7—'iam redit et Virgo, redeunt Saturnia regna,'
'And now justice returns, **Satan's ['Saturn' in Latin] reign returns**';'

8—'iam nova progenies caelo demittitur alto.'
'**now a new lineage is sent down from high heaven ['the gods'— *fallen angels*].**'

The *Sibylline Books* remained in the *temple of satan ['Saturn']* on *Capitoline Hill* until they were supposedly 'destroyed' by the 'fires' of yet another engineered social implosion. But many sources cite that the Sibyl's predictive program is now hidden away in the archives of the Vatican—a notion which corresponds with Michelangelo's disturbing painting of the 'six-knuckled,' apocalyptic, 'prophetess'-giant, on the ceiling of *the Vatican's* version of the temple of Apollo.

A variant of yet *another* phrase attributed to Virgil, '*e pluribus unum,*' was used in 'his' poem *Moretum;* and, as you know, this Virgil phrase also now graces our one dollar bill, in the form of a banner clutched in the beak of the rising eagle. This rising eagle (our society) wears a breastplate donning 12 vertical stripes instead of the Jewels which had been attached to the real Holy Breastplate; which likely represents a 'striped' 12 Tribes of Israel (remembering that stripes in The Bible represent enslavement). I would like to remind you that the translation reads, *'out of many, one'*—the appearance of this Virgil-quote beneath a 'Tower of Babel,' on our basic unit of currency is even further confirmation that early America too shared Nimrod's despotic vision. And we've now filled his ancient orders by creating **One World** from our many scattered nations of Israel—hence the name: **One World** Trade Center.

It is the numbers at the base of this pyramid on our dollar bill which reveal the dreadful purpose of this 'novus orddo seclorum' ('new world order'); these numbers read 1776 in, **Roman**, Numerals, which is a blatant proclamation, from America's very architects, that she was *founded* as the fifth and final Rome. And we've now *filled* Nimrod's ancient orders by creating this **One World** Order from our many scattered nations of Israel, which are represented by the bricks making up the pyramid—hence the name of this precious new temple: **One World** Trade Center. In a strange coincidence, Nimrod's new temple to 'Apollo' is, *1776* feet tall—matching the Roman Numerals on the one dollar bill, under *Nimrod's pyramid*. Finally, the print chosen for every book, magazine, newspaper, and even The Bible—in early America—were all typed in a font which was prophetically named, 'Times **New Roman**'—but another in an endless procession of, *'signs of the times.'*

As stated prior, *Virgil, like Nimrod,* was 'a man whose hand has now reached our own times, from thousands of years in the past.' **One World Trade Center**—Apollo's breathtaking new temple—has risen and the pope's precious Roman Empire will rise again right behind it. The destroyer of Revelation **9:11**—*the final Roman emperor and antichrist*—will soon come to power right before our very eyes! The good news is: All of these signs point to the fact that *Christ too* will be here before we know it.

33. Predictive Programming

Michelangelo's Cumaean *Sibyl—prophetess—*is painted on the ceiling of an institution whose very name, *Vatican*, means 'tellers of the future' ; *fortune telling* becomes quite easy when you *create* the future. In other words, you script and create conflicts—*wars and financial cycles*—with predictable outcomes, the clues of which are placed in pop culture, years in advance, in order to counterfeit one of YHWH's greatest tools for communicating with man: fulfilled prophecy, also known as the 'signs and wonders' spoken-of in the Bible.

Today this apparent phenomenon is called 'predictive programming.' Predictive programming, to the untrained eye appears as *phenomenal* since current events seem to be displayed in artwork and other pop culture in advance. Up to this point in our adventure, we've witnessed evidence of predictive programming preceding events ranging from coins featuring Alexander the Great as Apollo *the destroyer*—prior to Alexander's rampage—to 'mythology's' predictions of the temples of Apollo which followed horrible events such as 9/11. In this chapter we will explore this phenomenon a bit further.

For example: A fella named Morgan Robertson penned a book which foretold the sinking of the Titanic 14 years before it capsized. In his work, *Fu-

tility, or the Wreck of the Titan, Robertson's version of the Titanic rammed an iceberg, in April, at around midnight; this was nearly the same time and month as the Titanic was sank—*which also did so off the coast of Newfoundland.* Nearly the same specs as the **Titan**ic, the **Titan** was 800 feet long, had 3 propellers, 2 masts, a 3000 passenger capacity, and it was *British* owned. The Titan, too, was billed as 'unsinkable,' and the poor passengers on this fictional Titanic also ran out of lifeboats. And, as discussed, a 'Titan'—the name of both of these 'unsinkable' vessels—is a Greek *giant* who is, *half man, half 'god.'* (Some etymologies even connect the word 'titan' with the evolution of the name, 'satan.')

In *this* calamity, on screen and in circulated accounts, a creepy orchestra continued playing from their setlist until the Titanic disappeared in the sea. This stinky story, too, seems to be *more* spittle in the public eye, since it was their beloved *Nero* who continued playing *his* fiddle as Rome *burned to the ground*, just as did the band aboard the scuttled Titanic as she inhaled *her* last great gulp of saltwater; the creepy fiddle story is merely more homage paid to their precious Rome.

Eyewitness reports differ concerning the last song played by the band as the Titanic slipped into her watery grave but, the running story cites that they finished with a hymn titled, *Nearer, My God, To Thee*, which is about *'Jacob's Ladder'*—the Bible account describing the mechanism which *creates* 'titans.' *Wallace Hartley's* Violin, *which was no Strad,* was supposedly fished from the briny Atlantic during the mayhem; and in 2006, Hartley's eldritch violin fetched 1.7 million American dollars at auction.

The looming events of *Armageddon* were again recently highlighted, by every news source on the planet, when they heralded the astronomical events of **9/23/2017**, which seemed to be a perfect description of Revelation Chapter 12. *Eerily*, on **9/15/2017**—*just days prior*—the 4 Billion dollar Cassini space craft, *named for an* **Italian** *'engineer'*—was *crashed* into the hexagonal 'eye of Saturn,' by NASA. The *hexagon* is *highly* revered in sacred geometry; and, in case you forgot, the *temple of saturn* was a shrine built to *satan* upon *Capitoline Hill*, in Rome, **Italy**. The last verse in the passage below, **found in Revelation Chapter 9**, corresponds with the date on which 'Cassini' 'crashed' into the eye of satan—*9:15* :

> King James Version (KJV)
> **11 And they had a king over them, which is the angel of the bottomless pit, whose name in the Hebrew tongue is Abaddon, but in the Greek tongue hath his name Apollyon.**
> **12 One woe is past; and, behold, there come two woes more hereafter.**
> **13 And the sixth angel sounded, and I heard a voice from the four horns of the golden altar which is before God,**
> **14 Saying to the sixth angel which had the trumpet, Loose the four angels which are bound in the great river Euphrates.**
> **15 And the four angels were loosed, which were prepared for an hour, and a day, and a month, and a year, for to slay the third part of men.**

Cassini's special **9/15** delivery date, which was preceded by a *long* voyage to the hexagonal eye of satan, *could* double as a representation of the '**star**' described in Revelation **9:1-2**, which 'fell from heaven unto earth.' Remember, *'Lucifer'*—who *'fell from heaven unto earth,' once before—means, 'bringer of light.'* (Note: ironically, the Titanic was owned by '**White Star**' Lines) It took Cassini nearly 20 years, to the month, to arrive at the eye of Saturn; so, was Cassini's, long, calculated, trip, set to the hands of some, ancient, astrological clock of destruction, in order to—*at the perfect astrological time*—deliver some sort of 'keys to the bottomless pit,' to satan? It certainly seems like more than a coincidence that these two events occurred within five days of each other. And, as a result, can we now surmise that satan himself has arrived here on earth?

Perhaps Lucifer got right to work on **10/1** at the (Revelation) **9:1 Harvest** festival in 'Sin City.' Could this event have been only the first of satan's many, prophetic, mass-human-sacrifices to be made during his short visit here on earth? The fact that a large, lighted, hexagonal, eye—*an exact mirror image of the eye of satan on Saturn*—intermittently stared at the crowd from a stage in front of which victims bled to death, seems to substantiate this notion.

This hexagonal shape is even incorporated into Aldean's new logo, which made for the perfect backdrop for a mass-human-sacrifice. Aldean's logo boasts a single hexagram which is accentuated by the outline of three more hexagrams. Since the hexagram has six sides, this 'award-winning' stage lighting was flashing 666 before the sacrifice. The hexagram has been used in saturn worship for thousands of years, long before 'the eye of saturn' storm-phenomenon formed on the surface of the planet, which is a profound revelation. Remarkably, the eye of satan is 8,600 miles in diameter, in contrast to the earth which has a 7,900 mile diameter; meaning that, this 'bottomless pit' is just big enough to *swallow* earth, with roughly a few hundred miles to spare on each side.

I'm quite sure that we will be seeing many more of these hexagons in pop culture from now on; they are a celebration of satan's entrance into this world, in our times: It is a *sign* of the times—the supposed, *'new age.'* Keep a lookout for these, and especially the onset of logos incorporating a grouping of three hexagrams, denoting the number 666. Hexagrams, cubes, *and* pentagrams are closely related in Solomonic magic; they are the most powerful 'seals' for summoning demons. For a crash course in hexagonal symbology, and to gain a better understanding of its relation to the occult, there are entire documentaries dedicated to this 'sacred geometry' and these 'magical' properties.

The pyramid at *Luxor—standing in front of the trapped crowd in Vegas—* also displayed an impressive beam of light stretching to the heavens from its capstone; *this imagery doubles as the image on our one dollar bill!* I would also like to point out that an obelisk witnessed the Vegas murders, just as the one at the Vatican had witnessed those of Peter and Paul. If you've google imaged these items, I would encourage you to compare the suggested imagery with a final image, of a pair of light beams which stretched to the heavens from Ground Zero, immediately after the towers collapsed. All of this imagery demonstrates the sinister signature of the 'bringer of light,' *Lucifer—the sun god, Apollo.*

The events of 9/11 were predicted in the 'Back to the *Future'* movies, *and,* in dozens of other, movies, magazines, and album covers...including Busta Rhymes' 1997 album, titled, 'When Disaster Strikes.' *When Disaster Strikes,* was released a mere four years before the events of 9/11 unfolded. The art on the DVD features a sinister-looking Busta, laughing hysterically, while displaying two fingers, representing the Twin Towers. Busta's next album, 'The Coming,' released in 1997, predicts the rise of an antichrist: 'coming' soon, *to a city near you.* The album art for this heretical work features Busta **staring in a mirror**, dressed like a Catholic priest; fortune telling with the aid of a mirror is known as **'scrying'**—*which, again, is the very meaning of the word 'Vatican.' These creeps are 'telling' us of our own programmed future!*

All of Busta's heresy can be viewed by watching a video, titled, 'Pepsi Threatens Apocalypse,' on my new YouTube channel, *Judah Vision, https://www.youtube.com/watch?v=8EFGnrqU5oM. In which,* an 'Extinction Level Event' was tossed right in our faces during a 2018 Pepsi/Doritos SuperBowl commercial, just as the looming, contrived, sinking of the Titanic was dangled in the faces of our ancestors toward the end of the 19th century, *14 years before the Titanic was built and sank.* In the video link, I dismantle the symbolism in this apocalyptic SuperBowl commercial, and the striking message therein will be shocking in light of our studies today.

Pepsico's predictive commercial showcases a 'rap battle' pitting 'fire' against 'ice' as the Vatican's final solution to 'overpopulation.' At the end of this piece, **Peter** Dinklage *breathes* fire. *Saint* **Peter** was brutally executed by the Romans on the front stoop of Saint **Peter's** Basilica, and then buried *beneath* the temple in Vatican City—*the same ritual was practiced before the construction of the temple of satan on Capitoline Hill, just as the necromantic relics of* **9/11** *were planted beneath One World Trade Center.*

But if the truth be known…the 'tellers of the future' *also* have an entire necropolis buried beneath the foundations of *their* temple! This ancient cemetery is the result of **Nero's** Circus—*the sports event at which* **Peter** *and Paul*, along with *countless* other Christians who left their blood on this dirt, *were killed.* These are the very same terrible events which were mentioned in Revelation 17:6 :

6 And I saw the woman drunken with the blood of the saints, and with the blood of the martyrs of Jesus: and when I saw her, I wondered with great admiration.

With special permission granted from time-to-time by the *Fabbrica di San Pietro*, you too can visit the Vatican's precious city of dead Christians. Disturbingly, *visits to the remains of Peter and the early Christians—who were killed just outside the door of this joint—are organized according to the schedule set by the* **Excavations** *Office (ad nauseam).*

The ancient prophecies of Malachy, *Archbishop of Armagh*, predict a '**Petrus** Romanus' who would be the 'final pope'—these signs should be taken quite seriously. Especially since the title that pope 'Francis' has chosen can also be translated to *'***Peter** *the Roman.'* This fact makes the

Pepsi Threatens Apocalypse video even more creepy, since a **Peter** (Dinklage) is the fire breathing destroyer in *that* message too.

Adding to the fiasco, a statue of *Apollo—the destroyer of Revelation **9:11***—stands right next to the image of Busta Rhymes, in the Pepsi commercial. And, just like Nero in the burning of Rome—*and the fiddler on the Titanic*—Busta is playing an intoxicating tune on his flute while flames engulf the entire room! *So*, can *we* commoners expect the same *Fire and Fury?* Which doubles as the title of the new tell-all book about Donald Trump. This same 'fire and fury' predictive programming theme seems evident in the whole '**Stormy Daniels**' scandal since the Old Testament 'sun god,' *Baal*, doubled as a '**storm** god,' which explains the name for the mission 'Operation Desert **Storm**,' and, monikers like, '**Stormin**' Norman.' And let us not forget that, **Daniels**, is the Bible Book which, along with its sister-Book Revelation, warns of *our* looming apocalypse.

It appears that the demons working through this Council of **Nine**, who are utilized for the dirty work of burning cities and countries to the ground, are once again being conjured-up for the greatest predictive programming event ever conspired: *Armageddon! And*, it's not by mere coincidence that the pope's Knights Templar—the early version of the *Jesuit Order—who did the same during the Crusades, was also formed from **9** men*. This, evil, spiritual, ancient program of destruction, was uploaded from Roman to American architecture, to the operational dynamics of all of our governmental branches, to our educational system, and now you know that this evil even lurks within the vessels of the so-called 'men' who run *Hollyweird,* America, Britain, and the Catholic 'Church.'

From the Sibyl in Michelangelo's painting to the Titanic to the predictions of 9/11, the sons of darkness just can't resist showing us our own horrible fates, just before they imitate the ultimate acts of playing god: *predicting the future, and spinning the keys which unlock the doors to both life and death.* But, 'predictive programming' is little more than a counterfeiting of the breathtaking, fulfilled, prophecies in *God's Word.*

It seems that America's 'opioid epidemic,' too, was predicted thousands of years before *our* particular scene in this ancient puppet show: Aside from *destruction*, Apollo *the destroyer* is known as the 'god of medicine.' Which explains America's insatiable appetite for drugs (both, legal *and* illegal), our bulging prisons (modern-day slavery) as a result of over-regulated chemical substances which Nixon named the 'Drug War,' and our slow motion pharmaceutical commercials that fuel a whole host of invented ailments which, prior to the DSM, the DEA, our FDA, and the MAHF— *Medical Advertising Hall of Fame—never existed!* So, perhaps *the destroyer* has already been warming up for this calamity, and we never even noticed.

The return of *the destroyer* of Revelation **9:11** —*one of the Roman 'Council of Nine'*—was foretold by the Book of Revelation, the Cumaean Sibyl, the teachings of the satanic 'bible,' in the writings of countless other cultures around the world, and now it appears that the Vatican, *and Michelangelo*, were both in-the-know for this greatest of all conspiracies. *Unfortunately for America*, all of the evidence points to *Capitol Hill* as being the new home of this, old, sleeping, giant.

It also seems that this, ancient, 'Council of **Nine**,' are now pulling the levers behind the curtains of *our* so-called, 'shadow government.' Soon, just as the same men did with Jerusalem, Troy, Rome, Nazi Germany— *and every other collection of chiseled rubble on this planet*—America's credit rating will be reduced, our towering mountain of debt will be called, and the events thereafter will cause 'mens' hearts' to 'fail them for fear.' Most Americans, *naively*, believe that we can fight our way out of this debacle but this idea is the very catalyst which will kick off the greatest cataclysm since the dawn of man.

If you haven't already made the connection, Verginia's death symbolized the sacrifice that the consul of decemvirs made by burning down their precious Troy. The instructions for which were, undoubtedly, written in the Cumaean Sibyl's predictive script, handed down to the wicked men of earth by satan himself. And, remember, Constantine, too, quoted a long passage from the Sibyl's 'prophetic' book in *his* inaugural address, in York. Which shows that these 'instructions' have been followed diligently by every evolution of the same evil despots, throughout time.

34. Revelation 2:7

In the story of Athena's birth, Zeus swallowed the goddess of deep thought, Metis, in order to thwart a prophecy which stated that Athena would give birth to a child who would destroy Zeus and take his throne... *So*, Zeus swallowed Metis while she was still pregnant with Athena, to prevent this prophetic dethroning.

The above section expresses satan's will to prevent Christ from taking his precious throne on earth....Though the characters are *quite*-obviously different in his molested version of Revelation.

A few days later, Zeus had a splitting headache which he developed from a constant pounding which wouldn't escape him. He cleaved his head open in frustration and Athena sprung out, fully formed and clad in the armor she had been hammering upon inside her father's head. And, just as prophecy stated, Athena *was* more powerful than Zeus—**satan**.

This section of the satanic 'bible,' which is passed to 'little Suzy' at your neighborhood school, shows satan's ignorant belief that somehow the 'god of strategic warfare,' *Athena*, will arrive in place of Christ—*this is the antichrist*. This account is *satan's* version of the end, in which, *he wins*. But, if you know the Bible, you know that he will get his just deserts.

A *giant* eighteen foot statue of Athena, who now stands atop the Capitol Dome, is dressed in full *Native American* armor. If you've studied the slaughtering of our Natives at any length, it is clear that *the destroyer* was hard at work, once again, when the French, the Spanish, and the British— *fractured Rome*—first arrived on these shores. *This* fulfilled bit of 'predictive programming' lets us know that Greek 'mythology' is more like a horrific script for an *Extinction Level Event. Disturbingly,* Athena—*the statue atop the Capitol Dome*—is the goddess of 'building cities,' *along with* strategic warfare; as was *Nimrod,* who was also **18 feet tall** according to the *Epic of Gilgamesh.*

Athena, *who is also known for her wisdom*, has a pet **owl**. In celebration of the American government's worship of Athena's owl, the lawns and sidewalks surrounding the Capitol are arranged in the shape of a giant horned owl. You really should google image an aerial shot of this disaster. This explains why talking owls have now appeared in our culture, and are being featured on television peddling everything from Tootsie Roll Pops to eyeglasses.

Our presidents, academics, and CEO's, are now worshipping the stone owl of Athena, in **Bohemian** *Grove California*. It seems that the old Canaanite abomination of erecting an inanimate object for which to bow down and worship has also been revived in its literal form. And, it is no coincidence that along with the temple of Apollo, a 'grove' surrounded the cave of the *Cumaean Sibyl* who Michelangelo depicted as a ***giant***. Remarkably, **Bohemian** *means* '**giant**,' the stone owl worshipped in 'the grove' is ***giant***, and the owl is surrounded by ***giant*** Redwood trees.

The creeps who have rebuilt this ancient 'abomination of desolation' even burn a human **baby**—*a word which stems from the dedication of all new members of ancient* **Baby**-*lon to satan*—as a sacrifice to the ultimate antichrist, who now stands atop the Capitol Dome in DC. Worshippers at Bohemian Grove *claim* that the swaddled infant is merely burnt *'in effigy,' which may or may not quail your fears*. 'Ragnar Redbeard,' the pseudonymous author who wrote what many consider to be the awful forerunner to Anton Lavey's *satanic bible, Might is Right,* offers a cursory explanation for the mechanics behind these long-distance human-sacrifices-in-'effigy' when he writes:

> 'Innumerable are the folk-lore legends, relating to ancient and modern man-eaters. Formal human sacrifices upon the Alters of Idols are quite common. In Mexico and Ancient Britain, prelates butchered their victims (generally young virgins) in public, amid the acclaim of musical instruments, the chanting of beautiful liturgies, and the hosanna shouts of the mob.
>
> 'The modern prelate does not employ the rude smoking gully-knife, but uses other weapons, ten times more keen and more destructive. For every human sacrifice 'offered-up' in olden times, millions are offered now.'

Note: *Might is Right*—penned by a British Royal in disguise using a fake ancestral viking name who, held high-office in many lands on many continents under *multiple* assumed aliases, and whom helped catalyze multiple *controlled conflicts*—was published in 1890, so imagine what 'keen' and 'more destructive' high-tech methods for making their precious sacrifices that these pagans have today!

This is another book which, *like Lavey's,* can be terrible to read but offers a reader great insight into an ancient evil tribe of men who've been terrorizing mankind from the advent of Cain, son of Adam and Eve, who smote his brother Able, representing the world's first human sacrifice.

The ceremony at Bohemian Grove is nearly identical to the one described in The Biblical account of the Ten Commandments, in which the Children of Israel began to worship the golden calf. The timeworn ceremony is called the '**Cremation of Care**.' *Below are a couple of passages which speak to this ancient tradition* :

1 Kings 14:15 King James Version (KJV)
15 For the Lord shall smite Israel, as a reed is shaken in the water, and he shall root up Israel out of this good land, which he gave to their fathers, **and shall scatter them beyond the river** ['the grove' lies next to the ***Russian*** River], **because they have made their *groves*, provoking the Lord to anger.**

Jeremiah 32 King James Version (KJV)

35 And they built the high places of Baal, which are in the valley of the son of Hinnom, **to cause their sons and their daughters to pass through the fire unto Molech**; which I commanded them not, neither came it into my mind, that they should do this abomination, to cause *Judah* to sin.

These ancient rituals go hand-in-glove with, city building, oppression, and human slavery; *we* do all of the heavy lifting so the favored races of all colors—*race originally meant bloodline*—don't have to.

Below is the Biblical account which tells of the Whore of Babylon. Revelation 17, enjoy :

King James Version (KJV)
1 And there came one of the seven angels which had the seven vials, and talked with me, saying unto me, Come hither; **I will shew unto thee the judgment of the great whore that sitteth upon many waters**:
2 With whom the kings of the earth have committed fornication, and the inhabitants of the earth have been made drunk with the wine of her fornication.
3 So he carried me away in the spirit into the wilderness: and I saw a woman sit upon a scarlet coloured beast [Britain], full of names of blasphemy, having seven heads and ten horns.
4 And * **the woman was arrayed in purple and scarlet colour**, and decked with gold and precious stones and pearls, having a

golden cup in her hand full of abominations and filthiness of her fornication:

5 And upon her forehead was a name written, **Mystery, Babylon The Great**, The Mother Of Harlots And Abominations Of The Earth.

6 And **I saw the woman drunken with the blood of the saints, and with the blood of the martyrs of Jesus**: and when I saw her, I wondered with great admiration.

7 And the angel said unto me, Wherefore didst thou marvel? I will tell thee the mystery of the woman, and of the beast that carrieth her, which hath the seven heads and ten horns.

8 The **beast that thou sawest was, and is not; and shall ascend out of the bottomless pit, and go into perdition**: and they that dwell on the earth shall wonder, whose names were not written in the book of life from the foundation of the world, **when they behold the beast that was, and is not, and yet is.**

9 And here is the mind which hath wisdom. **The seven heads are *SEVEN MOUNTAINS*, *on which the woman sitteth*.**

In Revelation 17:18, John identifies the 'woman sitting on the beast' when he says : 'And the woman which thou sawest is that great city, **which reigneth over the kings of the earth**.' Just like the **Capitoline Hill** of Rome, *our* **Capitol Hill** is set upon one of seven hills in the City of Washington DC, a district which has *also* come to be known as the *City of Seven Hills!* What's more: New York City, *and Washington DC*, each—*or* both combined—could be identified as this: ***'city on many waters.'***

The *Library of Congress* boasts a behemoth mosaic of *Athena*. In this image, [1] **rays of sun flow across Athena's back (Apollo [Nimrod] was the 'sun god'** and his temples were always associated with Athena), and a miniature statue which looks like her and, [2] *stands upon the moon*, is situated to her left. Google this image and then look at the striking resemblance between the numbered bold sentences above and the corresponding bold sentences in the verse below. Revelation 12 :

> King James Version (KJV)
> 12 And there appeared a great wonder in heaven; [1] **a woman clothed with the sun**, and [2] **the moon under her feet**, and upon her head a crown of twelve stars: 2 And she being with child cried, [3] **travailing in birth, and pained to be delivered**.

A shrine to **Artemis** *shared* the complex surrounding the Cumaean Sibyl's cave and temple of *Apollo (the 'destroyer' of Revelation 9:11)*. Artemis, is Athena's half-sister, *who is the goddess of the moon* [2, above], the **hunt** (like the 'mighty hunter,' Nimrod Genesis 10:9), the **wilderness** (Revelation 17:3), **childbirth** [3, above], and **virginity** (Virginia).

In the very same mosaic of Athena, featured at the Library of Congress, I would like to point out that * '**the woman was arrayed in purple and scarlet colour**,' exactly as stated in Revelation 17:4. **Athena is holding a spear similar to the one which pierced Yeshua's side in her right hand** *which symbolizes that she 'killed god'* (John 19:34), which is the same claim that Nimrod made. **Athena's pet owl is again standing faithfully to her right, who America's leaders now worship in a** *grove*.

And, finally, **Athena is unfurling a scroll in her other hand** (Revelation 10:2)!

As with the Mosaic of Athena who now stands at the *Library* of Congress, **Legend cites that the *Cumaean Sibyl* 'always held a book in her hand'** ; and, as stated, *the oracular responses therein were 'then transferred to the Senate'* to receive the Sibyl's prophetic instructions in 'times of trouble.' Michelangelo's version of the Sibyl, who now sits on the ceiling of the Sistine Chapel, clasps this same horrible book with the six-fingered 'fist' which started our journey. **Sibyl's clutched volume foretells of *our* terrible end of times.**

The Statue of Liberty is *another* 'lady'-*giant* **who always *holds a book in her left hand* which we now know foretells the end of days; in most artistic renditions, the Sibyl is also pictured holding this book in her left hand.** ('Lady Liberty' was gifted to America by Freemasons in France —*home of the Knights Templar)* The base of the *Statue of Liberty* boasts a poem, titled, *The New Colossus,* in remembrance of the *Colossus of Rhodes—another, ancient, giant, depiction of Apollo (King Nimrod), and one of the Seven Ancient Wonders of the World—whose number was called long ago.*

I don't know how I could be the first to ever notice this but: The 'Statue of Liberty' is, literally, Alexander the Great—*the model for the Greek image of Apollo*—in a dress! This makes sense, since Apollo was known to parade in drag; he was a *transvestite*. Google image the 'face of Statue of Liberty' and, 'British Museum Marble Head of Alexander the Great,' and you will see that these two artistic renditions are identical! Look at the eyes and lips....Every line and shadow is Identical!

Remember, too, that Apollo was a 'sun god,' which is why the transvestite-colossus across the bay from the new Temple, of this sun 'god,' has seven sun rays beaming from his head. Apollo's special number is...*seven,* and to match this theme, the Book of Revelation describes 'seven bowls' from which he pours out seven 'woes' upon mankind. And finally, his torch represents 'Prometheus,' the 'mythological' Greek version of Nimrod who 'gave man fire' ; making him 'Lucifer' the 'bringer of light.'

John of Patmos, who wrote the Book of Revelation, would've been very familiar with these stories, since this 'mythological' cycle of destruction was running near its event horizon during his days. As aforementioned, 'these "mystery religions" of the ancient times were really no "mystery" to the men who wrote the New Testament.' This is why I believe that John repeatedly states, 'here is wisdom,' in Revelation: All of the information needed to break his code in Revelation was, a general understanding of the dark side's precious satanic bible—*Greek mythology, which we are handed in school at a young age*—the statues and artwork which he knew would adorn 'Mystery Babylon,' *and The Bible itself.*

I don't advise this but the scripture below illustrates how God ordered the Israelites to handle *these* 'places upon the **hills**,' *after* they'd destroyed every single person inside these horrible cities of baby murderers. Deuteronomy 12 :

King James Version (KJV)

**2 Ye shall utterly destroy all the places, *wherein the nations which ye shall possess served their gods*, upon the high mountains, and *upon the hills*, and under every green tree:
3 And ye shall overthrow their altars, and break their *pillars*, and burn their *groves* with fire; and ye shall hew down the graven images of their gods, and destroy the names of them out of that place.**

And now you know why the 'dust on your Bible is so thick'....This old scam threatens everything these vampires hold sacred. Again, I don't condone this for the Capitol Building; this scripture is only meant to illustrate what *could* become of us if we don't change our ways. Below is a song which was sung by the Twelve Tribes as they **eliminated** societies stuck in the finality of this same insidious behavior. Psalm 115 :

King James Version (KJV)
2 Wherefore should the heathen say, Where is now their God?
3 But our God is in the heavens: he hath done whatsoever he hath pleased.
4 Their idols are silver and gold, the work of mens' hands.
5 They have mouths, but they speak not: eyes have they, but they see not:
6 They have ears, but they hear not: noses have they, but they smell not:
7 They have hands, but they handle not: feet have they, but they walk not: neither speak they through their throat.

8 They that make them are like unto them; *so is every one that trusteth in them*.

The second half of verse 8, above, shows that burying your head in the sand will not be enough to 'save your bacon.' Lucky for you, '**The Living God**' *does* have the ability to accept apologies. Revelation 7 :

King James Version (KJV)
2 And I saw another angel ascending from the east, having the seal of the living God: and he cried with a loud voice to the four angels, to whom it was given to hurt the earth and the sea, 3 Saying, **Hurt not the earth, neither the sea, nor the trees, till we have sealed the servants of our God in their foreheads.**

I would get started on that whole 'apology' thing, right away, if I were you. This is the cycle of sorrow—these *are* the *'stones of emptiness.'*

35. Counterfeit New Jerusalem

After another series of grievous, contrived events, the sons of darkness will force our *Antithesis* which will be WWIII—the Synthesis of which, they *believe*, will be the *New Jerusalem*—counterfeited from Revelation 21 :

> King James Version (KJV)
> **21** And I saw a new heaven and a new earth: for the first heaven and the first earth were passed away; and there was no more sea.
> **2** And **I John saw the holy city**, **new Jerusalem**, coming down from God out of heaven, prepared as a bride adorned for her husband.

The counterfeiters of God's Word truly believe they will win this final battle of Good vs Evil. The sons of darkness believe that they are going to pave the streets with *your* gold as described in Revelation. The excess resources and technology which was robbed and stashed away from you will form an amazing utopia in which the Royal bloodlines believe they will live, free from pain, disease, work, or worry of any kind. The ruling elite are planning the elimination of all *religion*, *countries*, and, therefore, *wars*....After which, they will live happily ever after. Their plans have even been documented in granite, in another piece of 'predictive programming' which they refer to as: the *Georgia Guidestones*, which are near, **Athens**, Georgia. *They are deceived.*

If you listen to the song '*imagine,*' it describes this 'utopia' letter-for-letter, and now, we are calling people protected under the DACA movement, 'dreamers'—*wow!* Perhaps this is what Lennon's 'Bed-In' at the *Fairmont,The Queen Elizabeth in Montreal*, was all about. Lennon's *Bed-In* protest was supposedly a personal statement in which he stayed in the bed of his hotel as a non-violent 'protest against wars.' *So*, maybe Lennon had just uncovered some of his relatives' ugly plans to eliminate the 'dreamers' ; I hate to think of this but, Lennon's 'awakening' may be why he was shot in front of his home in New York City.

We have served as high-tech slaves—*the modern day pyramid builders.* The resources of the entire planet have now been mapped, mined, and hoarded for 'The Order,' by we slaves. The Strategic Petroleum **Reserve** (SPR) holds 20 Billion Dollars worth of **emergency** fuel storage of petroleum, which is stored underground in the states of Louisiana and Texas, by the United States Department of Energy. The Svalbard Global Seed Vault aka the Arctic Seed Bank, is chock full of non-hybrid seeds with which to replenish organic, life-sustaining food instead of the mutant hybrids we are offered by the Nazi seed company **Monsanto**, today. The pet name for this seed vault? *Noah's Ark!*

Elaborate underground bunkers have been built in order to protect the royal bloodline when the lights go out; these bunkers were designed to house all of the Washington elite, in the case of a situation like the burning of Troy. Meanwhile, *we* are piled on top of one another in cities, to make the job of extinguishing the slaves far easier, after we are of no more use to them.

Whence the gig is up and the curtains around the puppet show have dropped, revealing the long, red arms, wearing one of the faces of our *two-party* political system on each hand, it will signal a global event which they **are** prepared for, and we **are not**. And their greatest magic trick of all? They've turned all of your hard-earned labor into worthless paper; they've traded everything you own for absolutely nothing. They believe that they will ride away on their colored horses and that we will be left to explode into flames.

'Scattering' the inhabitants of earth allowed all of Nimrod's successors to manipulate markets, trade, and war, between these isolated nations. Our nations are now governed by a dark central force, *as one world*. There are only a few holdouts—North Korea and Iran being the main culprits—and it looks like we are attempting to subdue them now. This is all that's holding back this age-old cycle of destruction.

36. The Threshing Floor

In the end, this long bloodline of failed kingship combined with the Temple which was always misused in step with said monarchy, have been YHWH's proving grounds; a rich man only knows a new friend if, *when met*, they *don't* know he's rich. Just as David purchased the **threshing floor** on which to build God's **Temple**, so has the Temple been used to grind YHWH's people down to their very essence and separate them according to their worth. After the *grain* is reduced from the *chaff*, we are counted and weighed.

I am reminded of what was said by Yeshua in his parable of the **Wheat and the Tares**. Matthew 13 :

> King James Version (KJV)
> **24** Another parable put he forth unto them, saying, The kingdom of heaven is likened unto a man which sowed good seed in his field:
> **25** But while men slept, his enemy came and sowed tares among the wheat, and went his way.
> **26** But when the blade was sprung up, and brought forth fruit, then appeared the tares also.

27 So the servants of the householder came and said unto him, Sir, didst not thou sow good seed in thy field? from whence then hath it tares?

28 He said unto them, An enemy hath done this. The servants said unto him, Wilt thou then that we go and gather them up?

29 But he said, Nay; lest while ye gather up the tares, ye root up also the wheat with them.

30 Let both grow together until the harvest: and in the time of harvest I will say to the *reapers* [origin of the 'Grim Reaper' archetype], **Gather ye together first the tares, and bind them in bundles to burn them**: but *gather the wheat into my barn*.

YHWH *is* the underground river which feeds His people in Jerusalem from the *Spring* of *Gihon*; most of us simply haven't yet discovered *Hezekiah's Tunnel*. And it's a shame because it is a magnificent account and YHWH is a goodly ruler of his people whom He has adored since day one; unfortunately, we have done nothing but reject our sweet maker. YHWH vies for our attention and we rarely even turn around. He is there, if only you wish to find Him and once you do, your life will never be the same. It is bliss to put all of your worries in the hands of such a powerful King. He is the creator of the multiverse.

The sons of darkness have followed close behind the Great One and counterfeited every single thing He's made, done, said, and been called. So why wouldn't the evil ones come right behind Yeshua, **the *only* God to *ever* walk this earth**, to try and take His place, *also*?

The many sieges and actions against the tiny town of Jerusalem, throughout time, have all been the same ugly force: from Nebuchadnezzar's knights to the Romans who killed Yeshua to the viking kings to William the Conquerer to the Knights Templar and the Crusades, to East India Company, to the meddling being had between America and Jerusalem, today ; it is all the same bloodline of people fighting over the same strip of land and the same High Priesthood!

The common denominator between all of the above institutions is thus: The crusading Templar who searched for The Grail called themselves the '**Poor**' Soldiers of Christ; the sons of darkness mentioned in the Dead Sea Scrolls referred to themselves as 'The **Poor**,' and East India Company employed the same mechanism of amassing fortune for the purpose of world dominion; *EIC* called it, a '***corporation***.' Their own, precious, King Solomon snitches on this group again in Proverbs when he condemns this practice and identifies the forerunners of the Knights Templar, right in The Holy Word. Proverbs 1 :

> King James Version (KJV)
> **10** My son, if sinners entice thee, consent thou not.
> **11 If they say, Come with us, let us lay wait for blood, let us lurk privily for the innocent without cause**:
> **12** Let us swallow them up alive as the grave; and whole, as those that go down into the pit:
> **13 We shall find all precious substance, we shall fill our houses with spoil**:
> **14** *Cast in thy lot among us*; *let us all have one purse*:

15 My son, walk not thou in the way with them; refrain thy foot from their path:
16 For their feet run to evil, and make haste to shed blood.
17 Surely in vain the net is spread in the sight of any bird.
18 And they lay wait for their own blood; they lurk privily for their own lives.
19 So are the ways of every one that is greedy of gain; which taketh away the life of the owners thereof.

In more recent times, the practitioners of the same 'casting in thy lot' to form 'one purse,' program, can be identified by 'their fruits,' as The Bible states. Members of Skull and Bones are ordered to bequeath most of their great fortunes back to The Order's trust—*The Russell Trust Association*, whose financial books are even off-limits to the *IRS*.

We have observed the very same behavior with Royal blood-liners like *Warren Buffet*, who supposedly 'convinced' **158** Billionaires to Join Buffett and Gates in 'donating' their great fortunes for 'philanthropic purposes.' Believe me when I tell you that they are *not* 'donating' their precious billions in the name of good will; this is merely satan calling back what is his, to reinvest in the continuation of his despotic plan. Like everything else satan does and says, it is only a temporary illusion—*a lie*—and it's sad that people fall for this old scam, and that, in the end, they've lost their money *and* their souls. Let us not forget that the Clintons were nearly broke when *they* were chosen as financial collections agents for the same cause of evil.

This practice of combining and snowballing fortunes for the purpose of world dominion is as old as time itself; these people are of the same bloodline as the Knights Templar and are repeating the same financial practices, for the same depraved purposes. Matthew 7 :

> King James Version (KJV)
> **13** Enter ye in at the strait gate: **for wide is the gate, and broad is the way, that leadeth to destruction, and *many* there be which go** in thereat:
> **14** Because **strait is the gate, and narrow is the way, which leadeth unto life, and *few* there be that find it.**
> **15 Beware of false prophets, which come to you in sheep's clothing, but inwardly they are ravening wolves.**
> **16 *Ye shall know them by their fruits*.** Do men gather grapes of thorns, or figs of **thistles**?

'*Ragnar Redbeard*'—once again, the author of *Might is Right*—uses this Biblical metaphor of the '**thistle**' (above, in verse 16) while shedding light upon this same technology of a secretive group who hoards wealth while subversively ruling from the shadows, when he stated the following over 100 years ago:

> 'Is it not a fact that in actual life, the ballot-box votes of ten million subjective personalities are as **thistle** down in the balance, **when weighed against the far seeing thought, *and material prowess of*, say, ten strong silent men?**'

'Redbeards' use of the word thistle, above is an obvious and blasphemous reference to the above-mentioned scriptural accounts, in which the Bible drops the dime on this ancient cabal.

These men of all different colors and faiths are fighting over the same small town in the middle of nowhere! They are all digging, fighting, killing and conquering to steal the *High Priesthood* of the ancient Israelites—the *Holy Grail* that was strapped around Moses's brother's neck. *But we all messed it up:* From the kings which Yeshua reluctantly allowed to rule Judah, to the priests of the Temple for which he was hesitant to enter, *we all goofed it up!* And now things are so out of joint that once again our 'teachers need teachers' and *our 'rabbis need rabbis.'*

This is why it is so important that you put your life in the hands of Yeshua, and that you fill your vessel with **Good** and not with that which is **Evil**: with Christ, life becomes worth living and people wish to have what you have when you are free and understand the true message of His Word. Christ walked into the Temple which had become a 'synagogue of satan' and angrily flipped over the money changers' tables; Yeshua was 'blowing the whistle' on this entire great conspiracy to which we've all now turned our backs.

In a world where Christ knew that His act against the Sanhedrin and the Romans would blow the top off of their selfish scam, this **poor** carpenter walked into the streets of Jerusalem and healed the blind, brought life to the dead and spread a message which was *so powerful* that it marks the very point in time by which we have all set our calendars—**BC, Before**

Christ, and ***AD*** which stands for ***in the year of Our Lord***. And now these things too have been changed **by descendants of the same Roman liars who killed Christ and who are now attempting to steal your soul**!

Should we fight the system and the evil kings? No! We should just keep this big secret, held safely, close to our hearts, and share it whenever it's safe....Yeshua answered this question for us when he said in John 18 :

> King James Version (KJV)
> **33** Then Pilate entered into the judgment hall again, and called Jesus, and said unto him, Art thou the King of the Jews?
> **34** Jesus answered him, Sayest thou this thing of thyself, or did others tell it thee of me?
> **35** Pilate answered, Am I a Jew? Thine own nation and the chief priests have delivered thee unto me: what hast thou done?
> **36** Jesus answered, **My kingdom is not of this world: if my kingdom were of this world, then would my servants fight, that I should not be delivered to the Jews: but now is my kingdom not from hence.**

In ancient times, a scroll which had writing on 'both sides' was a title deed for land; in the Book of Revelation, after telling of a mysterious 'book' which has 'writing' on 'both sides,' in *Revelation 5*, John tells us *how* we are going to get our 'inheritance' back from the evil ones, when it states the following in Chapter 6 :

King James Version (KJV)

14 And the heaven departed as a scroll when it is rolled together; and every mountain and island were moved out of their places.

15 And the kings of the earth, and the great men, and the rich men, and the chief captains, and the mighty men, and every bondman, and every free man, hid themselves in the dens and in the rocks of the mountains;

16 And said to the mountains and rocks, Fall on us, and hide us from the face of him that sitteth on the throne, and from the wrath of the Lamb:

17 For the great day of his wrath is come; and who shall be able to stand?

We have a front row seat to the conclusion of the greatest drama ever to unfold, when our High Priest comes and, *by force this time*, takes back His Throne before His people. The Book of Hebrews spends *most* of its lines explaining that Christ has taken back the elusive *Holy Grail, The High Priesthood*, by *The Order* of *Melchizedek*. Look at Hebrews 7 :

King James Version (KJV)

22 By so much was **Jesus made a surety of a better testament.**
23 And they truly were many priests, because **they were not suffered to continue by reason of death:**
24 But this man, because he continueth ever, hath an unchangeable priesthood.

25 Wherefore he is able also to save them to the uttermost that come unto God by him, seeing he ever liveth to make intercession for them.
26 For such an high priest became us, who is holy, harmless, undefiled, separate from sinners, and made higher than the heavens;
27 Who needeth not daily, as those high priests, to offer up sacrifice, first for his own sins, and then for the people's: for this he did once, when he offered up himself.
28 For the law maketh men high priests which have infirmity; but the word of the oath, which was since the law, maketh *the* **Son,** *who is consecrated for evermore*.

When David told Nathan that he wanted to 'build' YHWH a 'house,' YHWH told Nathan that He was happy living in 'curtains' ; YHWH was right where He had loved to be—*living among His people*. And if you still *aren't* convinced that YHWH isn't crazy about King Solomon's Temple of Doom, *Revelation* clears this matter up for all of us when John sees the *New Jerusalem* descending from the Heavens. Look at Revelation 21 :

King James Version (KJV)
22 And I saw no temple therein: for the Lord God Almighty and the Lamb *are* **the temple of it.**
23 And the city had no need of the sun [Apollo was the 'sun god'], **neither of the moon** [Artemis was the 'moon god'], **to shine in it: for** *the glory of God did lighten it*, *and the Lamb is the light thereof*.

The *counterfeit* legend of the supposed 'Holy' Grail—*the molested cup version*—cites that, *if drank from*, it will impart upon its drinker, '*everlasting life.*' This too was stolen from you by the evil ones, for Christ *only*, who offers *true* everlasting life, *is* the Holy Grail.

I will see you there!

37. Amazing Grace

John Newton was a slave trader for East India Company who began his career on the sea in the British navy. On a voyage home from delivering a load of slaves, Newton's ship was enveloped in a violent storm off the coast of Ireland which nearly scuttled his vessel. While sloshing around, desperate and out of options, Newton prayed to the Hebrew God Yeshua and some cargo miraculously shifted to fill a void in the deck, lending the vessel stability. Newton truly believed that Yeshua had saved his life.

Newton began to view his captives with a more sympathetic view after his horrific experience, even becoming an ordained minister. Newton wrote 280 hymns to accompany his services, among which was his hit classic, *Amazing Grace*.

Many years later, Newton renounced slavery which was very unpopular for the day. He then wrote *Thoughts Upon the Slave Trade*. The tract blew the whistle on the horrific conditions these slaves were subjected to and Newton apologized for making his public statement so many years after himself participating in the trade: 'It will always be a subject of humiliating reflection to me, that I was once an active instrument in a business at which my heart now shudders.'

Newton's writing was so popular that it was reprinted many times over and delivered to all of Parliament. Afterward, MP William Wilberforce worked feverishly toward the English civil government outlawing slavery in Great Britain. Finally, in 1807, Newton lived to see slavery abolished, dying in December of the same year.

East India Company and 'Darwinism'

The Galapagos Islands were a popular stop along East India Company trade routes with which Newton would've been very familiar. EIC's weary sailors would *wonder* at the sight of the colorful diversity of animal life which inhabit the islands still today; it was an opportunity for these sailors to snack on them too. The Islands were known for their giant tortoises which are affectionately named after their home—*the Galapagos Tortoise*.

Since the animals were immobile when flipped upside down, combined with their ability to live without food or water for long spans of time, the sailors would load their decks with the tortoises to be used as food in preparation for months at sea. Darwin himself took a giant tortoise as a pet and it just recently made headline news when it passed away in 2006; 'Harriet,' was estimated to be 175 years old at the time of her death.

The abundant life on EIC's favorite pitstop Island of Galapagos also made for the perfect backdrop to their new invention of 'Evolution.' Actually, I'm sorry, I take that back....We *did* just learn that *evolution* was a *Roman* invention, didn't we?

Ahem....*I'm sorry*, 'Charles Darwin's idea' of evolution was plagiarized from a colleague of Darwin's who was compensated for his textual collection of ignorance in the form of **East India** Railroad Company stock. Darwin was then sent to India by EIC to learn the evil ways of this ancient Roman scam under the *tutelage* of East India Co. In India, there is *still* a festival named in Darwin's honor.

Darwin returned from India with 'his' fictionalized book, *On the Origin of Species by Means of Natural Selection,* or **the Preservation of Favoured Races in the Struggle for Life**.' This pirated book was created by EIC to remove God from *our* society, just as Nimrod did to *his*, in order to persuade the masses that eugenics was an *acceptable* practice...And, it worked. What followed was a modern-day system of antichrist and the euthanasia of millions of victims allover the world; and this evil creed also caused the deaths of millions of soldiers who were sent as the solution to a conflict by the very same wicked men who invented it.

East India Company and their dupe, Charles Darwin, may have fooled the whole world into believing that they evolved from monkeys which later led to the gassing and burning of the Nazi Germans' own neighbors but, there was one person who Darwin simply couldn't convince of EIC's recycled garbage teachings: his sweet wife, Emma.

You see, Emma never believed Darwin for a minute. And, despite all of his ignorance, Emma drug a reluctant 'Charlie' to church every Sunday until the day he died.

'Amazing' things happen when you truly begin to believe and crave every single Word of God—when you crawl out of the cave of deceit and finally begin to walk 'Upright'—the whole everlasting life thing is just an incredibly dumbfounding bonus.

38. Jedidiah Knights

We have all heard that George Lucas's films have amazing parallels to Greek mythology, the stereotypical 'hero's journey,' or even the messianic overtones one reads in multiple literary works. But George Lucas's incredible sense of esoteric symbology may run *much* deeper than previously imagined.

As discussed, Lucas's feature film *Raiders of the Lost Ark* spotlighted the Jewish treasure, the *Ark of the Covenant. And*, we've discussed the irony of the 'Hebrew treasure,' of which the hero is in pursuit, having sat *right beside* the *Biblical figure who actually wore the Holy Grail—the Breastplate of Judgment*—dangling around his neck.

But, what if I told you that Lucas's film franchise—*Star Wars*—threw the Grail *right in your face?* What if the Ark was featured in *one* of Lucas's movies, and another Hebrew treasure—*the Holy Grail*—was a central feature of his *other* blockbuster film series? Well, that is *exactly* what I am telling you. But, first, let us look at some of the many disgusting similarities between the Old Testament figures and objects which Lucas threw right in your face :

—Princes **Leia**: **Leah** became Jacob's wife through a deception on the part of her **father**, Laban. Princes Leah's father was another dark and 'deceptive' fellow: *Darth Vader.*

—**Anakin Skywalker**: This was **Darth Vader's** real name: *Anak* means 'Giant' in Hebrew. And **dearth** was a word used in The Bible to indicate **famine**: 'There was **dearth** in the land.' So, Darth Vader's name literally translates to ***Famine Giant***, *or,* ***Giant who causes famine***. The very first famine mentioned in The Bible was in the Joseph account where he predicted 'dearth' in the land after interpreting Pharaoh's dream and, therefore, the kingdom stored grain enough to profit handsomely from the prediction; sadly, since then, man has encouraged this process for profit.

The ancestry of the Biblical tribe of **Anakim** can be traced back to **Anak**, the son of **Arba** (Joshua 15:13; 21:11); at the time, **Arba** was thought of as the 'greatest man among the **Anakim**' (Joshua 14:15). When the twelve Israelite spies returned from their recon mission to the Promised Land, they fearfully reported of a 'people great and tall' whom they identified as the sons of **Anak** (Deuteronomy 9:2).

—'**Skywalker**' : **Skywalker** was the family name in the Star Wars series; ***Skywalker*** corresponds with the word ***Anunnaki***, which means, ***those who from Heaven to Earth came***. So, ***Skywalker*** = ***those who from Heaven to Earth came***. The ***Anunnaki*** were 'the gods' of ancient Babylon! They were also called the ***Anuna gods*** in the older Babylonian writings. These are the same beings which were worshipped by Nebuchadnezzar and his ancestors, who all had 'wings' and 'claws of an eagle,' just like the King himself began to grow in the wilderness. These were indeed the fallen angels described in Genesis.

The kings of Babylon were said to have been descendants of 'the gods,' and in all of the stone images found there, the kings towered over the other people depicted on the reliefs. Scientists are *also* baffled with the planetary information found on these tablets. Many of the planets and systems depicted in ancient Babylonian artwork weren't even discovered until the last several centuries.

—**Han Solo**: Han Solo was named for an ancient Babylonian, Hebrew scholar named **Honi**; *Honi* was infamous for 'drawing circles' in the sand in which he could pray to some dark '**force**' who would make it rain. Honi's most published and circulated story tells of an account in which there was **dearth** in the land and **Honi's** magic ended the famine.

On the royal families' heraldry—'*crest*'—the name **Honi** appears on the little cinched belt which is sandwiched between the two animals standing to each side of the *coat of arms*. The belt reads: '*shame on anyone who thinks ill of it* [evil]' ; this quote was used to describe '*hidden agendas*' by the French during the French Revolution; *William the Conquerer's Knights-Templar-relatives were also French*. The Russells' family crest—the founders of *Skull and Bones*—features the same garter and **Honi** inscription.

This 'cinched belt' has come to be known as a 'garter.' The Knights Templar wore these **garters** around their thighs when heading into battle. The *origin* of the 'garter' *also* comes from the prophetic Book of Revelation 19 :

> King James Version (KJV)
> **16** And he hath on his vesture and **on his thigh a name written, King Of Kings**, And Lord Of Lords.

The above symbolism is identical to that which is on the royal crest, save for the fact that the royal family, who are *related* to the Templar, chose to add the name of a Babylonian devil worshipper in lieu of '*King of Kings.*' The 'Order of the Garter' is the highest order in the royal family to which only **24 men** are members. Below is more goodness from the Book of Revelation 4 :

> King James Version (KJV)
> **4** And **round about the throne were four and twenty seats: and upon the seats I saw** *four and twenty* **elders sitting, clothed in white raiment; and they had on their heads crowns of gold.**

The Order of Skull and Bones has counterfeited the whole '**white raiment**' portion of this verse, too. Upon their induction into 'The Order,' they become possessed by demon 'gods' through a disgusting ritual using skulls to transfer these demons, after which they take on new names like, **Baal**, and then don their snazzy **white robes, which represent the 'purity'** of their newfound religion. The nine original Knights Templar were supposedly burned alive for the worship of heads and skulls of the dead, but this was more pacification for the truthers of those times; Donald Trump lends the same appearance of 'change.'

—Yoda: **Yoda** is the name of a **demon who is named in freemasonry literature**, aka 'Mephistopheles.' *This* 'Yoda,' appears to a practitioner of 'the craft' and helps him with advice, and, *if you will remember*, the *Star Wars Yoda* is the little fellow who imparts wisdom upon the characters in the movie. If you google image 'Yoda freemasonry Mephistopheles,' you will pull up the image of a fellow who looks identical to 'George Lucas's creation' in Star Wars. If you googled the image, I would like for you to notice that the 'practitioner' of this 'magic' is standing in one of Honi's 'circles.'

—Jedi Knight: **Jedidiah** is the Hebrew name for King Solomon of the Bible, and most of the raiders of the Holy Land, throughout time, have also referred to themselves as 'knights.' The 'Jedi' Knights all dressed like warrior monks even though they were in the 'future,' and the group fought with swords (light sabers) just like the Knights Templar—*even though they were in the future!* The Jesuits *and* the Knights Templar, *both*, consider themselves to be 'warrior monks.' *Jim 'Mad Dog' Mattis*, Trump's appointed Secretary of Defense, is also known as 'The Warrior Monk.' Among 'The Warrior Monk's' many disturbing quotes:

'It's quite fun to shoot them, you know. It's a hell of a hoot. It's fun to shoot some people.'

—**The Empire**: As with the British *Empire*, Star Wars is also centered-around an '**empire**' and the **logo for Star Wars,** as well as the words which roll in the beginning of the film, are bunched in the shape of a **pyramid missing its top**.

—**Death Star**: In the movie, **Star *Wars***, the ***Death Star*** is an artificial planet which can destroy other planets. Strangely, the **Anunnaki of ancient Babylon** told of a similar prophetic 'planet' : The ***Nibiru*** **cataclysm**, is a prophetic encounter between earth and a large planetary object which some groups, *even today*, believe will cause the end for our planet.

Nibiru, is a form of the ***Babylonian*** word, ***Nebuchadnezzar***—the **Babylonian king who *destroyed* the Temple of Solomon** in the Daniel account. And, '*Nebo*' is *yet another name for king Nimrod* who was depicted as a '**winged god**' in the times of Nebuchadnezzar's **Babylon**. If all of this 'winged-god'-talk sounds extremely familiar, perhaps one of the flunkies on 'Ancient Aliens' taught you the smokescreen-version of this account, *brought to you by* **Prometheus** Entertainment, which means, '***Nimrod*** *Entertainment.*'

Modern believers in the Judeo-Christian Bible are another such group who believe that a giant meteorite will end the war of Armageddon, whether they all know it *or not* ; in fact, **this interplanetary collision is *exactly* how The King James Bible, *ends!*** Revelation 18 :

   King James Version (KJV)

21 And a mighty angel took up a stone like a great millstone, and cast it into the sea, saying, Thus with violence shall that great city *Babylon* be thrown down, and shall be found no more at all.

The Vatican now owns a telescope in Northern Arizona with which many sources claim the group is carefully tracking an unknown object as it moves through space; the name of this appliance is, '*Lucifer.*'

Star-Gates
Lucifer was placed at the top of Mount Graham in Northern Arizona; this 'sacred ground' doubled as a 'star-gate' for the ancient Apache, and it functioned identically to those of the Sibyls' who spoke with Apollo. And, just as all of these temples to Apollo—scattered all around the world—were accompanied by untold dead human beings, the Vatican's new telescope, 'Lucifer,' too was built atop ancient burial grounds for these 'natives.' As you can imagine, a long and futile lawsuit preceded the construction of this abominable appliance.

From Apollo's 'gates of hell' to the Apache to every other society on earth who've *all* used these 'gates' to communicate with 'the destroyer,' these 'star-gates' stem from ancient Babylon; a name which, itself, as already established, means: '**Gate of God**.' Babylon's outer *'gates,'* through which city-goers would enter her walls, were each dedicated to a different *'god,'* so we can also gather that this 'star-gate' phenomenon is the very spiritual engine which powered Old Babylon. And that, symbolically, everyone who passed through these 'gates of god' themselves *became gods!* Remem-

ber, this is the very foundation of satanism also; men becoming god of their subjective universe! The Forbidden Fruit!

As we now know, Daniel is one such Brother who had surely passed through the *Ishtar Gate*. A Gate which was excavated in Babylon, and was moved along with satan's seat into the Pergamon Museum in Germany (Revelation 2:12-13), prior to Hitler's coup d'état, which was financed by Skull and Bones. It is public record that the US government seized assets controlled by Brown Brothers Harriman—heirs to the East India Co. dynasty of evil who had excavated and moved the Ishtar Gate, in the first place. US authorities seized these assets in the autumn of 1942, under the Trading with the Enemy act. Prescott Sheldon Bush (W's granddad) *was the senior partner for this wicked corporation.* W's dad, George Herbert Walker Bush, kicked off the Gulf War, and, W himself was in charge during 9/11 which resulted in Apollo's newest complex and star-gate— **One World** Trade Center. All of these men were members of the infamous order of Skull and Bones on Yale University.

Jacob's Star-Gate Dream

After *his* stairway to heaven dream, Jacob made an undeniable reference to these star-gates when he himself noted that the land of 'light'/'god' also seemed to be a 'gate to the gods.' Genesis 28 :

> [17] And **he was afraid, and said, How dreadful is this place**! This is none other but the house of god [Elohim: 'the gods'], and **this is the gate of heaven.**

And, finally, Christ himself speaks of these crazy *star-gates* in His following warning to all mankind! Matthew 7 :

> King James Version (KJV)
>
> **13 Enter ye in at the strait** *gate:* **for wide is the** *gate***, and broad is the way, that leadeth to** *destruction* **[***Apollo/Apollyon:* the 'destroyer' of Revelation 9:11], and *many* there be which go in thereat:
>
> **14 Because strait is the** *gate***, and narrow is the way, which leadeth unto life, and** *few* **there be that find it.**

The scripture above really comes to life when using the rightful word **Apollo**, in verse 13, which should state: Wide is the **gate**, and broad is the way, *that leadeth to Apollo…*' ! The verse above shows that The Bible clearly describes Apollo and his gates to hell, which were guarded by the demon-possessed Sibyls who now make their home on the Vatican ceiling.

It is no coincidence that the 'Golden Gate Bridge'—named for the famous gates through which Yeshua rode his donkey—was built upside-down and on the wrong side of the country in comparison with the Golden Gate to Jerusalem; haven't you ever wondered why the Golden Gate isn't, *'gold?'* It is also very fitting that this structure which leads to the world capitol of homosexuality, Bohemian Grove, the Bohemian Club, Burning Man, and Anton Lavey's original satanic 'church,' was made to be so terribly, *'wide' and 'broad'* (Mathew 7:13, above). I suppose that since California's 'state goddess' is 'Minerva,' *aka Athena—*Apollo's destructive cohort—then she would also double as the 'goddess' of New Babylon's Western Gate. And, since Athena had an owl as a sidekick, this also clears up any question as to why an *owl* is worshipped in Bohemian Grove.

This ancient **gate** symbolism explains to the observant and righteous servant, the precise reason that the 'Golden Gate' of Jerusalem was prophetically 'sealed-off' by the evil ones so many years ago: This event was meant to prevent Christ from, again, riding his donkey—customary for a king—through that very **gate** and taking back **his** throne from *the destroyer!* This is the reason Yeshua chose to arrive in Jerusalem through the Golden **Gate**!

In addition to the donkey symbolism, by riding through a *City Gate*, which were customarily dedicated to demon-gods, He was declaring Himself as *The One True God of all of Israel! Yeshua*, was symbolically speaking directly to the 'principalities,' 'powers,' 'spiritual wickedness in high places,' *and*, 'rulers of darkness of this world,'(Ephesians 6:12), to claim back Israel as His own! *PROFOUND!*

The 'star-gates' in 'Star Wars' were called 'Infinity Gates.' According to 'wookieepedia.com' :

> Through what the *Kwa* called the 'power of the cosmos,' **the Infinity Gates were able to transport them across the galaxy** or project devastating Infinity Waves. **The Gates were accessed from a Star Chamber, within massive pyramidal structures known as the Star Temples**. The Star Temples and its associated

buildings contained traps which protected the Chambers from intruders. **Inside the Star Chamber was a 'realm of infinity,' a pocket dimension that housed the central control station which was used to control the 'power of infinity.'**

Passage through these star-gates in *old* times were merely a one way proposition. But with the advent of the electronic revolution, it seems that the old 'bringer of light' may be doubling down on projects like CERN and Cassini, in order to convert these rusty old gates of hell—which in the past had simply served as interstellar phone booths—into wormholes through which the old 'dragon' might again make safe passage back to our world. And when he does—*which, he may already have*—we will once again find ourselves 'armpit deep' in an epic which will make 'Star Wars' look like a silent movie.

As endless as the goofy cast of characters in Star Wars is, I imagine that the entire Babylonian pantheon of ancient other-worldly 'gods' are celebrated through the fictional characters of this film. And we now pack up the family after 'church' to go watch the tales from the 'dark side' of The Bible, which celebrate the demon gods of ancient Babylon. If you google 'Christianity and Star Wars,' you will see that many Christians have even been so-deceived that they believe that the movie was *divinely inspired*. And many even use the 'messianic symbolism' in Star Wars by which to 'recruit' new Christians. Wow!

As hard as it may be for you to believe, 'Mystery Babylon' has now encompassed the entirety of our planet; meaning, Nimrod's ancient despotic plans to again enthrone a single man as sole ruler of the entire world have now been carried out by an evil trust which has defied the erosive nature of time—an evil which has creeped in to *destroy* our societies over-and-over again. And whether we refer to this event as, *the rise of the antichrist, Prometheus and the Eagle, the rise of the phoenix, the new age, the apocalypse, Armageddon, the new world order, novus ordo seclorum, age of Aquarius, the return of the Nephilim, the new Atlantis, the rise of the golden dawn, the morning of the magicians, anno satanas—year one of the rule of satan, the return of Apollo, the cosmic dance of shiva*, or by any other name, it is merely the return of the sun 'god': *the destroyer of Revelation 9:11*.

Solomon—*the builder of the original Temple*—again snitches on this evil system of becoming 'god,' in Ecclesiastes 1 :

> King James Version (KJV)
> **9 The thing that hath been, it is that which shall be; and that which is done is that which shall be done:** and **there is no new thing under the sun.**

That Solomon states of this recurring evil, **'there is no new thing under the sun,'** is an elusion to the very same **'rise of the sun god'**: Revelation 17:8's… beast that, '…**was, and is not;** and **shall ascend out of the bottomless pit**…'. These passages, along with *many* more Biblical prophecies which we don't have time to uncover, show that this cycle will repeat itself. Any day now, the 'beast' spoken-of by, John's Book of Revelation,

Anton Lavey, Apollo's Sibyl, and countless other accounts, will rear his ugly head.

It should now be quite clear to you why, the ancient, six-fingered *Giantess* clutching the book in which the 'sun god' *Apollo* outlined our inevitable destruction, was painted on the ceiling of the *Vatican...an institution which has stolen the Holy Grail—the High Priesthood of Christ!*

Oh... which reminds me: Before I go, we need to finish the business we started here: We need to identify the *Holy Grail* in the Star Wars 'epic'...

...Drumroll, *Please...*

The Holy Grail was strapped around Darth Vader's neck!

That's right, the *dark side has stolen the Holy Grail in film, too.* Haven't you ever noticed that Vader wears a 'chest plate' decorated with colorful buttons? If you google image the pictures of both a Jewish Cohen and Darth Vader, you will notice that they wear ephods which are nearly identical. And, believe it or not, the **'control panel'** on Vader's **chest plate** *is even inscribed with* **Hebrew** *lettering!*

When viewing a close-up of the imagery of the breastplate around Vader's neck, I would like for you to notice that Jacob's pillars stand to each side of the Star Wars version of the Grail, which has only nine buttons instead of the 12 Jewels which are attached to the Biblical Breastplate of Judgment. These 'pillars' stand to each side of the 9 'buttons' which represent the 9 knights Templar. This is the same powerful imagery which we see at the top of the **freemasonry hierarchy pyramid**: *a Knights Templar holding one end of a freemasonry banner and a freemason holding the other.* The image on the banner is the all-too-familiar *'compass and square'* of freemasonry.

And, now we will substantiate our suspicions that the Holy Breastplate *was* the 'object after which the Templar had lusted'.... On the same **freemasonry hierarchy pyramid**, the 'high priest of freemasonry' stands on Nimrod's pyramid, just beneath the one-eyed antichrist which is emitting rays of light. Now, look halfway down the right side of the pyramid and **you will notice that this gentleman is wearing the *entire*, Jewish, Priestly Ephod!** The Bible tells us that the ephod fell into the hands of those who began using the Breastplate of Judgment to communicate with the dark side, and the imagery on the freemasons'/Knights Templars' own publication confirms this fact. And just as The Bible displays the Holy Grail in plain sight, so does the pyramid of freemasonry—**standing on a Tower of Babel! Look again at this**!

And if that weren't enough proof that the Breastplate of Judgment *is* the Holy Grail, the Hebrew words which represent the action of the Holy Grail, **the words *'Urim* and *Thummim'* are inscribed on the school seal of... Yale University, home of the nefarious Order of Skull and Bones**. This illustrates that the Breastplate of Judgment truly *has* been stolen by the dark side and is still being used for the same baleful purposes! This is satan's demonstration that *he* has stolen Christ's High Priesthood. This abomination represents the pinnacle of man being 'god' of his subjective universe—*us. I know it's all very disturbing but, isn't it amazing?* That the Holy Grail is *now* being worn by the 'High Priesthood' of freemasonry, *the Order of Skull and Bones;* and being such ravenous 'wolves in sheeps' clothing,' who might be controlling, *them?*

I suppose the true *high priest* of the 'dark side' could be a naked, evil man in the bowels of a Scottish castle, laughing madly with horns gorilla-glued to his head. Or, perhaps, *she's* an anorexic cat-lady staring from a rain-drizzled window of a cluttered, ammonia-laden, loft on Fifth Avenue. But, I suppose that it really doesn't matter; it is only a matter of conjecture and the important thing to know is that it *has* been stolen from the good guys.

Oh....Wait a minute, just one more thing: I almost forgot about the 'hero' in Lucas's film. You already know that nearly every single shred of Star Wars has been dredged up from Babylon's leftover pantheon but, in all of the excitement, I almost forgot about our *old friend*, and starry-eyed hero, *Luke Skywalker!* Luke's symbolism is very simple....It seems that **Lucas, himself just** couldn't resist the age-old forbidden fruit of *becoming 'the god'* of *his* 'subjective universe,' when he named the central character in Star Wars *after himself:* '**Luke**.'

I suppose now that we've spent all this time together, you probably want some sort of advice from me? Huh? Well, there are a couple of items that I would certainly handle if I were you—*right away*—a mission: Save yourself first—*Romans 10:9, 10.* And after that, *save as many of the others as you can.*

And another thing which the 'dark side' in Hollywood has stolen from you....'May the Lord be with You!'

Thanks for listening,

Judah!

Chopped Sticks

They're a chair, or pair

Of Dutch footwear,

Father of Dogwood and the Rose,

Killer of Counts

Where Joan won't denounce,

After being bounced from the strings of her bows.

And it's funny how a *Strad*

found the finest of the trees,

Whilst wood that's found as fine as that

Makes the drabbest of piano keys.

It's fun to write about paupers;

We mostly do of kings;

Here *I write* to caution all

For which you use God's wooden things.

Judah—written around the age of 17

The Cross

It is highly intriguing, to me, that the *head* of every state and city around the world are *still* referred to as a province's 'capitol,' or, *head*—even though capitol means: *dead,* head. And I sometimes wonder if it's more than a coincidence that in the Gospels of Matthew and Mark the term *Calvary*, the location of the Crucifixion of Christ, is translated to mean, 'place of [the] skull,' which also doubles as the precious symbol of the Order of Skull and Bones on the sinister Yale University. Calvary, of course, is the place that human sacrifices were made for the Roman government.

The plus-sign-shaped cross which now graces flags allover the world also comes from this group of Hebrews; the book of Numbers describes how YHWH had ordered these nomads to setup camp in the shape of a Cross, at the intersection of which the mobile synagogue was placed right in its center. Ironically, this placed YHWH in the same position of the plus-sign-shaped Israelite camp as *Christ* would later be placed on the *wooden* Cross, at the hands of the Romans and the Jewish High Priest—His own appointed leader of the Hebrew Tribes.

The crucifixion of Christ marks the first and only time in history that these villains will ever actually 'kill' God. Christ went out as a 'Lamb' but, unfortunately for the evil ones, He will return as a *'Lion!'*

To read a more detailed account of the Russell family and their conquest of the New World, the Knights Templar and the Holy Grail, the Order of Skull and Bones, the Jesuits, the Freemasons, the royal family, the antichrist, or anything else in this book, please read my Amazon #1 Bestseller, Sacred Scroll of Seven Seals.

Also, if you enjoyed decoding the symbolism in this work, please click on the following link to visit my new YouTube Channel, Judah Vision (https://www.youtube.com/channel/UCPThv43NoCAQkGZvi0Wb5aQ), where I will keep you posted on the latest occult symbolism placed in popular culture media.

If you enjoyed this work, please give it a Five Star Review on Amazon!

Thanks…

Judah!

CPSIA information can be obtained
at www.ICGtesting.com
Printed in the USA
BVHW032043201218
536104BV00001B/187/P